Cave to Castle

How to transform any property business using

Customer Relationship Management (CRM)

By Atuksha Poonwassie, Charles

Eaton-Hennah and Haico Van der Steen

Copyright

Table of Contents

Preface

Atuksha, Charles and Haico provide CRM consultancy services through Focus 2020, a company that helps property investors, developers and entrepreneurs find, acquire and retain loyal customers. We understand the needs in this marketplace because we are also property investors and developers; our team have built up portfolios of rental properties, we have developed property for rent and sale including empty properties and we have run new-build and refurbishment projects. We have been trained by, and worked with, some of the biggest names in the industry, including Kevin Green, John Lee and Vincent Wong. In addition, we've got over 40 years of Customer Relationship Management (CRM) experience between us; experience gained from working with some of the world's best known brands as well as with some niche small businesses and property entrepreneurs.

As a result, we have a clear understanding of the importance of managing the critical relationships essential for successful property investors and developers, and we've created an approach that brings the benefits of CRM to this marketplace. We focus on the various components of CRM that are relevant to help you build and grow your business - whether you invest, source property deals for others, supply to the property industry or run property mentorship and seminar programs.

We know the strategies and technologies that can best help you create successful partnerships with your investors and trades, keep on top of all the deals you're working on, use social media and marketing techniques to grow your business, and track what works for you and what doesn't. There are a number of mistakes that companies make when implementing CRM that usually lead to increased costs and a low uptake of interaction. The information provided in this book will give you the best chance of making the most of CRM and believe us, the benefits are worth it!

If this is the first time that you are reading about CRM and how it can help your property business, we hope that this book gives you inspiration and ideas to improve the relationships you have with your customers and prospects. It may raise further questions, provide quick wins for your business and help you build a loyal customer base. We would love to hear your feedback and hear about your success stories. Our contact details can be found at the back of this book.

We wish you every success in growing your business and building long-lasting, happy customer relationships. This is an exciting marketplace and we truly believe that by setting up CRM correctly within your business from the outset, not only will your business grow faster but the foundations upon which it is built will be stronger. We hope you enjoy the book!

Acknowledgements

We are thankful to so many people who have helped us get this book to where it is today. Their insight, support and time has been invaluable in helping us shape the structure and content of this book.

In particular, we wish to thank the following people for sharing their thoughts with us through the CRM interviews conducted; In particular, Kevin Green, Kevin Green Wealth; John Lee and Vincent Wong, Wealth Dragons; Simon Zutshi, Property Investors Network; Juswant and Sylvia Rai, Berkshire Property Meet; Rob Warlow, Business Loan Services; Daniel Latto, Daniel Latto Coaching; Shaa Wasmund MBE, SW Media Enterprises; Lee Nicholls, Property Plus Wales; Davin Poonwassie, Simple Backing; Keith Penny, Pennymatters and Sunil C Patel, London Achievers.

We also wish to extend our thanks to The Prince's Trust, our team, clients, friends and family who have supported us through our journey. Your support has been invaluable.

Why We're Writing This Book

"A well-satisfied customer will bring the repeat sale that counts."
- James Cash Penney

For a few years now, major organisations have been talking about a new way of building a loyal, engaged customer base. It's called Customer Relationship Management, or CRM for short.

CRM is not just a corporate buzzword or marketing industry fad. Successful companies in all sectors have been using CRM to help them deliver great customer experiences and generate profitable revenue growth; companies like Lush Cosmetics, First Direct Bank, Apple and Costa Coffee.

We believe that it's not just big companies who should use CRM to drive their business forward. CRM is a way of doing business that puts your customers at the centre of everything you do – and it doesn't need complex technologies, big expensive computer systems or expensive staff to implement it successfully.

Like many successful business ideas, CRM has become a term widely used to describe many different activities, strategies, technologies and products. Some of these are truly innovative, some are simply a repackaging of the things successful businesses have always done, and some are attempts to ride the latest bandwagon.

Think of a local corner shop. The shop owner knows who his customers are because he sees them every day. He knows who his regular customers are and he knows those who come in just once in a while. As a result he can greet his regulars by name - he knows their usual purchases and if he introduces a new product line he will know which of his customers are likely to buy it. He also knows the customers that would prefer home delivery, or who need help with their packing. Because of the great service they get, his customers recommend the corner shop to their friends and neighbours, and because the shop owner knows where his customers live, he can use leaflet drops to let them know when he is running offers and promotions that will appeal to them. His knowledge of his customers' purchasing also allows him to carry the right lines and keep efficient stock levels.

This is CRM in action.

So why should all businesses consider CRM?   Simply put; customers are the lifeblood of any business. Without them, the business will fail, but treat them well and they stay.   And loyalty and advocacy is good for your business as loyal customers are better customers.   According to the Chartered Institute of Marketing, investing in retaining customers is between four and ten times cheaper than trying to attract new ones. It's a good business model; increasing revenues and reducing costs.

1. Loyal customers need less of your time to service
2. They complain much less often
3. They don't need lots of help in understanding your products and processes
4. They will keep buying from you and be more interested in other products and services you have
5. They will recommend your products and services to others, increasing your marketing reach
6. Your staff will be happier too; they much prefer dealing with happy customers to unhappy ones

"A customer is our lifeblood in any of the businesses that we run, so they are everything." - Kevin Green

Loyal customers can actually work as an advocate for your business and their testimonials and recommendations will help to attract more customers for you and from your competitors, growing your business' size and profitability.

We believe CRM allows a business to achieve this, and properly applied, can allow property investors and developers to do the same as the corner shop owner; even if you do not see your customers daily and have 000's of customers to service. We intend this book to show you how. We hope you find it interesting and useful. And we know that CRM can positively transform your business as we have seen over and over again.

Customer Fact
On average, loyal customers are worth up to 10 times as much as their original purchase – Customer Think

What is CRM?

"Every day we are saying, 'how can we keep the customer happy? How can we get ahead in innovation by doing this?'... Because if we don't, then somebody else will." - Bill Gates

The Many Definitions of CRM

CRM has many flavours. You'll see that while most industry experts and commentators talk of CRM as a business strategy whilst technology companies focus on the technology in their definitions. Here are some popular definitions of CRM:

"An enterprise wide business strategy designed to optimise profitability, revenue and customer satisfaction by organising the enterprise around customer segments, fostering customer-satisfying behaviours and linking processes from customers through suppliers" – **Gartner**

"A management philosophy according to which a company's goals can be best achieved through identification and satisfaction of the customers' stated and unstated needs and wants." – **Business Dictionary**

"Enterprise wide software applications that allow companies to manage every aspect of their relationship with a customer. The aim of these systems is to assist in the building of lasting customer relationships – to turn customer satisfaction into customer loyalty." – **Computing Dictionary**

"A widely implemented model for managing a company's interactions with customers, clients, and sales prospects" – **Wikipedia**

Cave to Castle

Our Definition of CRM is this:

Effective CRM comprises of four components that working together, let you put your customers at the heart of everything you do; Business Strategy, Activities, Tools and People.

1. **Business Strategy -** This is an on-going determination to keep your customers at the heart of everything you do. The strategy is like a road map of how this is going to be achieved and ties perfectly to your business objectives and aspirations.

2. **Activities -** These are the things the business does that add value to the customer; experiences that customers have every time they interact with the business, whether it's by phone, personal visit, email, or web.

3. **Tools -** These are the systems and technologies the business uses to allow it to deliver those experiences effortlessly and in a time-efficient manner.

4. **People -** These are the people involved in the business; from those defining the business strategy, to managing systems to providing front-line services and support. It is about ensuring that your teams have the right support and guidance to provide exceptional products and services to customers at every interaction.

It's important to emphasise these four complimentary and balancing aspects to successful CRM. Just implementing a new system, or doing email-marketing or setting up a customer service department is not enough; these are simply components of a much wider approach.

When we're talking to property people we quite often hear them refer to CRM as a system that can be added on to what they currently have. In particular they mention contact management and email marketing; where contact management is a database used for storing customer and prospect information and where email marketing is a system such as MailChimp or AWeber that they can use to send out emails. Our experience shows that these alone will not deliver all of the benefits the business is expecting even if you see growth in the short-term. It is not a stable foundation for future growth. You must first consider the bigger picture of what the business is trying to achieve and then develop activities to build a great and coherent customer experience. Successful CRM needs a total approach.

Say for example that you want to build a house. You start with the design, architecture, costs and planning aspects. Part of this will include defining the process for building; you employ the right teams, you may have a project manager on site who follows the plans and you know the stages the house build will take. Then you clear the land, dig the foundations and so on. So, if you were recommended a team of builders, would you use them without knowing what you were trying to build? We are sure the answer to this question is no.

So consider this: when it comes to CRM and business, there are too many companies who start with the tools (the builders) without having a strategy or plan in place. There are so many CRM technologies out there, there is no need to fit your business around the technology – it should be the other way round. You could end up compromising your business growth when there is no need to.

"CRM is about being able to manage your customer relationships, so as it says on the tin. It is much easier to keep a customer than find a new one. And it is about keeping in regular contact by providing relevant, valued-added information." – Davin Poonwassie

Why is CRM Important? The Changing World

Our world is changing at an ever-increasing speed. Consumer behaviour, often driven by fast developing technology, is changing faster than ever before. What is possible today was hardly dreamed of ten years ago. Consumers have access to more information, are more demanding and a lot more vocal. They are communicating in many new ways, from mobile telephony, SMS and email through to the internet and Social Media platforms such as Facebook, Twitter, YouTube, Pinterest, Instagram, TripAdvisor and Snapchat – all businesses that didn't exist in the early 2000s.

Those consumers are also quick to use Social Media for their own benefit. Now disappointed customers are as likely to complain about the business using Twitter or Facebook rather than through the business' customer service channels. This can make it very difficult for the business to either learn from it or indeed attempt to deal with the complaint. Remember, a customer is more likely to tell up to five times more people of a bad experience than a good one. Their experiences fly all over the world at the speed of light; make one mistake as a business and it will be broadcast to millions of people in a flash. A few years ago, Nikon published on a social media site that a good photograph was only good because of the camera and not the photographer. Within hours the news spread virally over the Internet; many of Nikon's loyal customers felt insulted and claimed to switch to Canon.

The explosion of digital communication has also set new norms for service. Consumers now expect businesses to be able to react and respond near to immediately, and leading companies such as Amazon and eBay have invested heavily to allow them to meet this demand. These rising consumer expectations now present all businesses with real challenges.

"I think we have to be more aware of our customers today, especially through Social Media." Kevin Green

At the same time, Regulatory demands are increasing. The wealth of data generated by new communication technologies mean businesses have to strictly adhere to legislation limiting how they deal, process and store customer information.

There is no way to turn back the clock and without any doubt the pace of change will continue. Businesses of today need to be sure they are up for meeting these challenges if they want to survive in tomorrow's market.

Cave to Castle

Customer Fact

Failure to respond to complaints or problems posted on Social Media channels can lead to a 15% increase in the churn rate of current customers – Gartner

How can CRM Work for Property Professionals?

"We see our customers as invited guests to a party and we are the hosts. It is our job every day to make every important aspect of the customer experience a little bit better." – Jeff Bezos

We've developed an approach to allow us to bring the benefits of CRM to the property market. We have a clear understanding of the needs and challenges of property investors and developers, and the key relationships involved in a successful enterprise. We've focussed on the various components of CRM and have identified the areas that will help you grow your business, whatever your property interest.

We understand those needs because we are also property investors and developers and understand this marketplace well. We have experience of Property Sourcing, Renovations, Building and Developing and bringing back to life empty homes. In addition, we also provide guidance and support to a number of property-related organisations such as renovation firms, HMO experts (Houses of Multiple Occupancy) and Independent Financial Advisors / Firms.

We often get asked about the practical benefits of adopting a CRM approach to business. There are many, but here are some of the more common ones:

1. CRM means you stay closer to your customers. It allows you to anticipate customer needs quickly; you can address issues before they become a serious problem, spot new opportunities, and pick-up on supplier problems before they affect your schedule.

2. Better client and customer relationships help generate new business via referrals, advocacy and testimonials

3. CRM allows you to grow your business faster and more steadily by helping you close the 'back door' – reducing the numbers of customers who leave (churn). Tenants stay longer increasing your occupancy rates, investors re-invest, suppliers go the extra mile & coaching clients stay to start joint ventures. Better relationships also mean fewer customers go to your competitors.

4. CRM systems allow you to store all your customer and prospect information in one place, whether they are tenants, investors, suppliers, motivated sellers, event attendees or mentorship candidates. This will make servicing them easier, more responsive and more relevant

5. It allows you to build and maintain a full history of your communication with each person so that anyone in your business knows what has been said and done for example:
    a. How many emails you have sent them and when
    b. Which properties they've viewed
    c. How often you had to send out rent reminders
    d. How many property deals they have done with you
    e. How much has someone invested with you
    f. How many events have they participated in such as which podcasts they have listened to and
    g. What seminars, coaching sessions and webinars they have attended?

6. CRM allows you to track the success of your sales and marketing campaigns whether you use email, social media, post or any other

channel, allowing you to fine tune your marketing for the future in order to make the customer experience better

7. CRM allows you to create simple, streamlined business processes that will free up time so that you can focus on leading the business rather than running it. It allows you to set appointments, schedule calls, receive automated alerts reminding you to follow up, and assign status codes for all your leads and deals, so you never miss an opportunity to stay in touch

8. And you can report on, analyze and profile all aspects of your customer data; for example - determining your most valuable customers so that you know where to focus and prioritize your resources. Remember Pareto's law that says 80% of your revenue is likely to come from 20% of your customers. You need to know which customers are within that 20%!

Customer Fact
By 2020, the customer experience will be more important than any other factor to consumers – Customers 2020 Report

Interview – Kevin Green
The Importance of Customers

We were lucky enough to spend some time with Kevin Green, property entrepreneur and Owner of Kevin Green Wealth. We took the opportunity to ask him about his route into the world of property investment, and how he uses a Customer strategy to help grow his business.

Like a lot of people who have made a business out of property, Kevin started out on a completely different career path – in his case dairy farming. It was only during a period of travelling that he decided that property was where his future lay, after meeting a number of people who were already in the industry. Now Kevin is one of the country's most successful private landlords with a portfolio mainly based in Wales, Scotland and Northern Ireland. After becoming successful in this area, he began to be invited to share his experiences with others, and about five years ago started his own training and mentoring programme.

However, while Kevin gets enormous satisfaction from his mentoring activities, property is still his core business, and he still enjoys creating homes for people to live in: "I love taking something stinky and smelly and turning it round into a nice place - and seeing the joy of people when they go in there - either tenants or the new owners, that does it for me".

When it comes to the role of his customers, Kevin is unequivocal, "A customer is our lifeblood in any of the businesses that we run and so they are everything. In our businesses, the customer always comes first". Kevin's CRM system is a big part of his business, enabling him to respond quickly and appropriately to issues that crop up; "Customer Relationship Management is number one and we have a system that we use here. So if we have a query or a complaint comes in from either a tenant or any other part of our business, we are back on that within 12 hours. We jump straight on it and sort that out."

Unusually, the CRM system that Kevin uses was developed in-house by one of his own team, and along with a Spreadsheet system runs the tenancy side of the business.

He emphasises that his customer centred approach isn't just about having good software; "We get the relevant people in place as and when needs be." But Kevin still keeps close tabs on the customers himself: "If there is a severe complaint, I get involved and I deal with the customer whether it leads to court or not. And they appreciate that."

He uses MailChimp email marketing to support the training and mentoring activities, and it works well "MailChimp allows us to group, mail market and hold different groups of people which is really all we need on the coaching and mentoring side." Email is the main method for communication, but Kevin is careful to use it in a way that adds value to the customer experience, rather than simply as a sales tool: We use the 80/20 rule there, where no more than 20% of our messages will be any form of sales orientation and at least 80% shall be content".

Kevin's also starting to use social media to open up another channel with his customers, and finds Twitter works well to help bring in customers for both the rental and mentoring businesses. He creates the content himself: "Twitter is the best for us but then I suppose I put the most time into it and because I like it, I am the one that posts on Twitter. Its only 140 characters and it's easy, simple, right up front and instant. That is what I like about it."

Web marketing also forms a major part of Kevin's communication activity, and is particularly successful in gaining new customers: "A lot more of our tenants actually find us through the web – and they tend to be a better class of tenant".

However, in these days of electronic communication and social media, it's really the personal touch that customers expect: "The best way is face to face and the second best way is telephone and the third is email. It's more personal. Although it takes a lot of time out, our customers appreciate it so we do focus on that when we can. We will answer a query especially if it is a complaint or an enquiry with an email but we will also follow up with a telephone call." When it comes to regular communication with his tenants, Kevin also employs a CRM approach, and asks all his new customers how they'd prefer to hear from him: "When we engage with the tenants, we ask which they would prefer – whether it is text, telephone or email and we will honour that then when we interact with them."

One of the biggest challenges Kevin sees facing any business with customers nowadays is responding fast enough to their demands. Consumers see that big businesses like Amazon are very quick to react and other businesses need to be able to do the same. He considers social media like Twitter as a way for businesses to find out what their customers area really thinking: "I see that all the big companies including ourselves need to answer queries or complaints much more quickly from customers. I think in the old days, a lot of companies could maybe respond at some time, but now it needs to be immediate or 'as soon as' because bad news can travel very fast and can affect your company majorly because people thrive on negativity unfortunately. I think that anyone who hasn't got a social media presence is missing out as they need to monitor what is going on there as well. "

Finally, we asked Kevin what his top three tips would be for anyone starting or growing their business. He replies: "Always be customer led, test your markets, and keep it very simple so that everyone can understand it."

Interview – Shaa Wasmund MBE
The Importance of Relationships

It was the BBC that called Shaa Wasmund a 'serial entrepreneur', something her CV proves without doubt. Plucked from her university course by boxer Chris Eubank as his PR, she started her first business, a PR Agency, at the age of 24. Since then she's set up a number of high profile enterprises, including property development and also found the time to write 2 bestselling books: "Stop Talking and Start Doing" and "Do Less, Get More".

We wanted to talk to Shaa about the importance of relationships in business so it was interesting to hear her answer to our question about what she enjoyed most about her business career; "Oh, without question, it's dealing with the people. It's working with the people I get to work with; whether they're people from my team, the people that come to my workshops, or the women who come to my The One Retreat. I'm lucky to do work I truly love!"

Shaa's interest in relationships extends to her attitude to her customers. Unlike many of the personalities we've talked to, her definition of customers doesn't include a financial transaction; "In my view a customer is anybody that I interact with at any point through my work. So that could be somebody who comes to my website; they're a customer. We don't have to have had a monetary transaction for them to be a customer. I believe that people who come to my website to read my blog are also customers."

When it comes to CRM, Shaa reiterates the importance of the personal aspects as opposed to simply seeing it as a technical exercise; "I think when Customer Relationship Management is shortened down to CRM it feels like a technical software solution. In reality CRM is about how you build relationships with your customers, and a relationship can't be built purely through software. That software might help you manage complex or multiple or many relationships, but actually it's how you interact with that person that builds your relationships with them."

Shaa's team uses InfusionSoft for managing email to their customers, both for Smarta and her mentoring business; but the way they use email reflects the difference in the customer bases: "For Smarta we use a more traditional marketing model using a standardised format and a structure. There is a newsletter that goes out each week as well as a set number of articles. Because my mentoring business is much more about my own personal relationship with customers then at Smarta, our marketing is much more aimed at building relationships. The content and structure of our messaging depends on what I'm doing, and what I can see the customers want. The smaller customer base lets me build one on one relationships as well as one too many. But with Smarta, it's always one to many."

She also touches on a point we like to make about adding value to your customers through the content of your marketing; "I'm a big believer in the give, give, give, ask approach. So we're constantly giving great content before we'd ever ask anyone if they want to join something that we're doing."

As you might expect, social media is well suited to Shaa's relationship-based marketing strategy' "I use Twitter, Facebook, and LinkedIn for different reasons. Facebook works well for events, if I put something up about The One Retreat, we'll usually have the next course filled up within 4-5 days. Twitter is great for reaching out and connecting with people as well. And it's really useful to use tracking to see what customers are doing."

Podcasts aren't something Shaa has ruled out doing in the future, but stresses the importance of making sure they are relevant for her customers; "I think like anything, there's no point just jumping on the podcast bandwagon because everybody else had done it. You should only really do podcasts because you have something interesting to say."

When we asked Shaa about future CRM trends she returns to her point about adding value and relevance: "It needs to be more personal, I think that is what everybody wants. And I think integrating social media in CRM is something that is going to become more and more commonplace for everybody. The best CRM that I know, use and love from a small business perspective is "Contactually" - I just love how easy it is to use.

Finally we asked her to give us her top three tips for any business thinking of introducing a CRM strategy: "First of all, introduce CRM to your business well before you think you need it, number one. Number two is listen! So if somebody has got a complaint, instead of automatically being defensive, listen. Because even if that person might be 80% wrong there's still 20% in there that's a nugget for you to help yourself and your business grow. So listen rather than be defensive. And thirdly build relationships, not customers."

Creating Your CRM Strategy

"It is not the employer who pays the wages. The employer only collects the money. It is the customer who pays the wages." – Henry Ford

As the old saying goes, a journey of a thousand miles starts with a single step. The journey for your business starts with creating a CRM strategy. This should set out your vision for the business, and the approach for achieving it. Defining this strategy means involving your team from the start, as they are the ones who will be implementing it and dealing with it in their daily operations. If the strategy is not clear or supported throughout the business, your CRM efforts will be wasted and you will not see the expected or required results.

Step 1: Be Clear About Your Business Objectives

Start by determining where you want your company to be in 3 to 5 years from now. Not all businesses are the same and what is good for one, may not work for another. We can't all be Apple, Nespresso or Coca Cola but don't be afraid to think big; you could be aiming for 500 properties, a £5 million turnover, tenants in 400 rooms, a £3million property development or running weekly training courses on property education. Whatever your aspirations, don't limit them. Evaluate whether your business objectives are realistic in context of your business model and the industry you operate in. If not, can changes be made to your business to still deliver your vision or do you need to re-address the vision?

Step 2: Get Customer-Centric; Put Yourself in Your Customers' Shoes

Once you're clear about your objectives, you need to put yourself in your customer's shoes. Evaluate your current customer experiences and decide if it it's sufficient. If not, come up with improvements that should be made to deliver a greater customer experience; for example, why not follow-up maintenance visits on rental property to ensure the tenant is happy with the supplier's service and the effectiveness of the work. Record the outcome, positive or negative, against both the tenant and the supplier. Spend time mapping all the customer touch-points (all the ways your customers and prospects interact with you, for example face to face, website, customer service call and so on) and customer processes within your organisation. Once you have done so, talk to your customers directly; ask them to score you on each of these. Ask them where your services could be improved, what their priorities are and how they prefer to be communicated to. What would make the biggest difference to them? If you have different types of customers, try to speak to representatives of each of the groups. If you can, run reports to identify your top customers and start by talking to this group if you have limited time. And when you go through this process make sure you involve your employees so they all hear what their customers have to say about your business and team.

Spend a lot of time listening to the people that you work with, as many of the best ideas will come from those who deal with customers every day – and they'll also know where inefficiencies in dealing with customers generates wasted effort. Listen twice as hard as talking – you have two ears and one mouth for a reason!

"Knowing more about your customers lets you create much more effective marketing." – Vincent Wong

Step 3: Start to Create a List of Activities (Tasks)

Begin to identify a list of the activities (or tasks) your business can undertake in order to create a great customer experience. For example, improve you the event registration process by sending a reminder email with all details two days before the event to reduce the number of non-attendance, try out more targeted communication with your clients to ensure they have the right amount of information at the right time, respond more quickly to enquiries and complaints both online and offline. Empower your customer facing staff to make instant decisions on complaints up to a certain value and give your team better technological support so that customer information is at their fingertips.

Step 4: Align Your CRM Activities to Your Business Objectives

By undertaking step 3, you will have created a whole list of areas where your business can improve the customer experience. You now need to evaluate whether implementing these changes are in-line with your business objectives for the longer term and whether you are committed to go the extra mile to deliver these changes. If you decide the changes are needed, you should go through the list of changes and evaluate the likely impact implementing these changes shall have on your systems and business practices. Some changes may be easy to implement but with only a little impact on the customer experience. Other changes may be more complex to implement but will have more dramatic results. While part of your planned improvement might be to purchase a CRM system that allows all of your team to know about all of your customers, be careful not to mistake a CRM system for a CRM strategy. A CRM strategy should be decided and a CRM system chosen that can implement the strategy.

When those responsible for creating what would become First Direct Bank first met, they all sat around a large table to decide how the new bank would work. <u>On the table was a single piece of paper, and on the paper was written the single word 'Customer'.</u>

Since starting out, First Direct has consistently been the bank with the most loyal customers.

Step 5: Set Your Priorities

With all the information and ideas you've gathered so far, it is time to start setting priorities and creating the first draft of your CRM strategy. When setting priorities you'll need to take into account costs, complexities, the returns they'll deliver to the business, as well as the impact of issues the business currently faces. For example if you've identified that you are losing customer information because you are writing details on small bits of paper or that messages are not being passed to you in your office, this may be your highest priority to address. Sometimes you will find there may be some low hanging fruit; activities which are easy to implement and which will show a benefit quite quickly. Others may require a huge investment in time or resources, are much more complex or are even unrealistic.

Balancing activities against benefits and costs can be a complex process. We suggest one straightforward methodology as follows;

1. Score all of the activities from 1-10 for **business benefit**

2. Then score each activity from 1-10 on **benefit (or value) to the customer**

3. Sum the scores and rank the activities with the highest score first.

Note that you might decide to weight one more than the other if say, business benefit is more important to you right now than the benefit to the customer. Ask another team member to score the same items so that you can check the perceived benefits are in keeping.

4. Then you'll need to apply scores estimating the **cost** and **complexity** associated with executing each activity and factor these in by creating two more scores. These are only based upon your best guess at this point and should not take too much time to do.

   Note that the ratings scores are an excellent way to start the debate and you can always decide to adjust scores as needed.

Some tasks might emerge that have high benefits and low costs and complexity. These will naturally figure highly on your final priority list. Conversely, high cost/complexity with low benefits will be at the bottom of your list. Your final decision over the position of each task on the list will need to balance benefits and costs/complexity, and the nature and realities of your particular organisation. If you have serious resource constraints then you will tend to prioritise low complexity tasks more highly. A business that is cash-strapped will naturally prioritise lower cost items.

Below is an example of what your CRM strategy document may look like. Please email us at marketing@focus2020 if you would like to receive an electronic version of the document. Be sure to send us your name and phone number. Alternatively, further contact details can be found at the back of this book.

Setting Priorities

Item Number	Area	Description	Business Benefit	Perceived Customer Benefit / Value	Business Benefit Score	Customer Benefit / Value Score	Cost Score	Complexity Score	Total Score
1	Data	All customer information in one place	Access for all from one system. No loss of information, no need to update multiple systems, time savings. No duplicate customer information.	Don't get multiple communications about products and services due to duplicate details. All information is correct	9	4	7	7	27
2	Sales and Marketing	Ability to capture leads from website direct to sales people	Quicker Response time, no loss of information, more efficient sales process	Quick response time	8	7	8	8	31
3	Sales and Marketing	Automated newsletter for B&W investors with latest deals	Close deals sooner, keep in regular contact with investor base	Timely information about deals, targeted communication based upon interest	6	9	9	9	33
4	Customer Service	Set alerts for follow-up calls with tenants to ensure all is OK with works	Better customer service	Better tenant satisfaction, more engagement, ability to deal with remaining issues faster	8	8	9	7	32
5	Customer Service	Customer services having access to full communication history to service calls	Resolving customer enquiries quicker and increased customer and staff satisfaction	All staff can access details immediately - no need to repeat information	9	8	9	7	33
6	Teams	Improve staff motivation and job satisfaction by empowering team	Reduction in staff sickness levels, more engagement and efficiencies	Consistency, familiarity, have a go-to person	9	9	9	9	36
7	Analysis / Reporting	Ability to identify top 20/30% of best clients in order to prioritise focus	Increase profitability, improve loyalty, prioritise workload	VIP treatment, are acknowledged as most valuable customers	9	9	8	7	33
8	Analysis / Reporting	Run analysis to determine profitability per customer and cost of conversion.	Provides insight to allow to focus on most profitable segments. Also shows more profitable segments for removal from business	Possible efficiency improvements on servicing the customer	8	4	7	6	25
9	Sales and Marketing	Increase prospect conversion by 10%	Increased Revenue, increased ROI	More targeted information to allow a quicker decision	8	5	7	6	26
10	Analysis / Reporting	Specify target groups for messaging purposes	Increased ROI, less wastage	Receiving relevant communication	6	8	8	6	28

Key:	Range	Meaning
Business Benefit	1 to 10	1 = Low Benefit, 10 = High Benefit
Customer Benefit	1 to 10	1 = Low Benefit, 10 = High Benefit
Cost Score	1 to 10	1 = High Cost, 10 = Low Cost
Complexity Score	1 to 10	1 = High Complexity, 10 = Low Complexity
Total Score	1 to 40	Consider the Higher scored opportunities first but review all of them in turn to ensure nothing is missed

Note: Most of the time, some of these scores will be weighted depending upon what is right for your business. This could be dependent upon whether you have more or less resources, finances etc. For example, if my budget was really tight, I may double all the values in the Cost Score column. This is a methodology that we find useful.

Step 6: Build Your Business Case

Make no mistake, developing and implementing a CRM strategy will require investment in your business, both in time and resources. However, the benefits will be substantial and shall ensure that your business is built on solid foundations.

Now that you have a prioritised list of activities you'll need to focus on the more detailed numbers for those items at the top of your list you want to take to the next stage. We'd recommend that all businesses spend time on this process to make sure the numbers work.

For each of the CRM activities planned, look at the revenue gains and cost savings you can expect, as well as overall costs. There are two types of costs to consider. The first is external such as software and systems installation costs, consultancy and outsourcers' fees and training costs. The second is internal such as staff time, office space and staff incentives. Increases in sales revenues might come from new customers, repeat business and more effective upselling or cross selling. Example of savings made as a result of CRM might be reduced marketing costs (due to better targeting and increased recommendations), reduced customer service costs as complaints decrease and processes get more streamlined, and reductions in staffing levels or overtime. One of our favourite wins for a customer of ours was an increase of $300,000 revenue for a single event that resulted from a change in the communication plan and the targeting without an increase in spend.

Look at these over a period of time – depending on when you need to see benefits; it might be three months or 6 months or even longer. We usually find it easier to break these down to a month- by-month basis.

Working out the benefits of some activities in terms of revenue can be difficult. Some activities may be dependent upon others, some will offer cost savings as well as revenue gains, some activities will require up-front investment, others might involve costs further down the line. Be realistic, but recognise that this is not an exact science and that you are likely to make revisions along the way. We've seen even big companies get their estimates wrong but in our experience, small business owners and property entrepreneurs usually have a pretty good feel for what is sensible and achievable.

The resulting CRM strategy document will support any requests that you may have to make for additional funding whether it is internal or external.

Step 7: Deep Dive into the Detail

This is the final step in creating a CRM strategy for your business. It is a deep dive into what has already been created and allows you to specify tasks, assign responsibilities, identify linked tasks (where one section may have to follow another) and assign timelines and milestones (identifying stages where a significant piece of work and can be signed off and closed).

Here, the first task is to start breaking down your activities into more manageable chunks. For example, when creating a single customer view, your smaller chunks could be to determine which data items and feeds you wish to use (such as a website feed, twitter feed, Excel spreadsheets, data from your financial system etc.). You will then also need to decide what data items you wish to collect, such as first name, surname, address, email address and so on. Next, assign an owner to every chunk and agree when this is to be done by. It could be that all chunks are assigned to one person but assign them anyway so that there is an official 'owner'. As some chunks are dependent upon others to be completed, ensure you review the strategy as a whole to make sure it still works. This part will move whilst the project is underway. This is normal as there will always be unforeseen issues that need to be factored in along the way.

This can also be viewed visually using a Gantt chart so that you have an instant view of it at a higher level. This is good for any presentations that you may have to do. An example of the CRM strategy and the corresponding Gantt chart (created in Excel) is shown below.

Please email us at marketing@focus2020 if you would like to receive an electronic version of the documents. Be sure to send us your name and phone number. Alternatively, further contact details can be found at the back of this book.

CRM Strategy

Priority Number	Area	Description	Item Number	Item Description	Status	Create Date	Current Owner	Target Completion Date	Closed Date	Comments/Resolution
1	Data	All customer information in one place	22	Determine data sources for consideration	Closed	09/05/2014	Anduka	29/05/2014	27/05/2014	
			26	Formats for data load	Open	11/05/2014	Charles	09/09/2014		
			27	Structure of database	Open	11/08/2014	Charles	29/09/2014		Out for review with business
			28	Data Cleansing Rules	Open	11/05/2014	Data Team	29/09/2014		
			29	Client Category Mapping	Open	11/05/2014	Anduka	09/09/2014		incomplete - needs further review
			31	Standardised job titles	Open	11/05/2014	Naico	09/09/2014		Need to speak to web designers and get costs
2	Sales and Marketing	Ability to capture leads from website direct to sales people	32	Create Page for Data Capture on Website	Open	11/05/2014	Naico	23/09/2014		Need to speak to web designers and get costs
			33	Define the information to be collected	Open	11/05/2014	Marketing	14/09/2014		
			34	List of Sales people to be included	Open	11/05/2014	Sales	09/09/2014		Need to confirm current list
4	Customer Service	Set alerts for follow-up calls with tenants to ensure all is OK with work	35	Set up alert functionality for use by business	Open	11/05/2014	Anduka	27/09/2014		
			36	Full Contractors list available	Closed	11/05/2014	Charles	23/09/2014	13/09/2014	
			37	Contact management to record outcomes	Open	11/05/2014	Anduka	09/10/2014		
6	Teams	Improve staff motivation and job satisfaction by empowering team	39	Run staff workshops to identify requirements	Closed	11/05/2014	Naico	02/09/2014	02/09/2014	
			40	Staff satisfaction survey	Open	11/05/2014	Naico			Survey to be launched on the 6th - waiting on covering letter
			41	Financial considerations	Open	11/05/2014	Board	29/09/2014		
			42	Follow-up processes for re-evaluation	Open	11/05/2014	Naico	09/12/2014		

Item Number	Item Description	Start	Days	Target Completion	Status	Number of Workers	08-Aug	09-Aug	10-Aug	11-Aug	12-Aug	13-Aug	14-Aug	15-Aug	16-Aug	17-Aug	18-Aug	19-Aug	20-Aug	21-Aug	22-Aug	23-Aug	24-Aug	25-Aug	26-Aug	27-Aug	28-Aug	29-Aug	30-Aug	31-Aug	01-Sep	02-Sep	03-Sep	04-Sep
	Data																																		
22	Determine data sources for consideration	09/09/2014	7.0	16/09/2014		2.0																													
26	Formats for data load	16/09/2014	12.0	29/09/2014		1.0																													
27	Structure of database	09/09/2014	20.0	29/09/2014		2.0																													
28	Data Cleansing Rules	11/08/2014	57.0	29/09/2014		1.0																													
29	Client Category Mapping	11/08/2014	23.0	09/09/2014		1.0																													
31	Standardised job rates	11/08/2014	23.0	09/09/2014		1.0																													
	Sales and Marketing																																		
32	Create Page for Data Capture on Website	14/09/2014	7.0	21/09/2014		1.0																													
33	Define the information to be collected	11/08/2014	28.0	14/09/2014		1.0																													
34	List of Sales people to be included	11/08/2014	23.0	09/09/2014		1.0																													
	Customer Service																																		
35	Set up alert functionality for use by business	11/08/2014	41.0	27/09/2014		1.0																													
36	Full Contractors list available	11/08/2014	10.0	21/08/2014		1.0																													
37	Contact management to record	11/08/2014	81.0	09/10/2014		1.0																													
	Teams																																		
39	Run staff workshops to identify requirements	11/08/2014	5.0	16/08/2014		2.0																													
40	Staff satisfaction survey	16/09/2014	23.0	09/09/2014		1.0																													
41	Financial considerations	11/08/2014	43.0	29/09/2014		1.5																													
42	Follow-up processes for re-evaluation	29/09/2014	79.0	09/12/2014		2.0																													

Key
On Track
Missed
Not On Track
Complete

Cave to Castle

Interview - Simon Zutshi
Understanding the Customer Journey

Simon started his career in property at an early age. After graduating from university and securing his first job as a Graduate Trainee at Cadbury Ltd, he purchased his first property in 1995. He then rented out two of the spare rooms in his home to two friends of his who were still at university. This covered the mortgage and so Simon pretty much lived for free. The money he was able to save from his job, and the extra money he make from a part time business promoting Student night club events, was enough to provide the deposit to purchase his second property in 1998. The first property was then let out to Students and has been ever since. Simon speeded up his investing such that he was able to leave full time work at Cadbury in 2001. Able to then fully focus on his property investing, by 2003 he had completely replaced the income he was previously earning in his full time job.

At this point Simon realised that, rather than make all of the property investing mistakes himself, it made a lot of sense to learn from other successful investors.

He went online to look for a property specific networking group but could not find any so he decided to start one himself.

That idea became the business that is now the Property Investors Network (PIN) and has been so popular that 12 years later there are now monthly meetings in over 50 locations across the UK. Simon's business also provides training and mentoring, including one of the most well respected courses in the industry, The Property Mastermind Program established in 2007.

Simon realised that communications with his members would be very important, and he started using CRM for this purpose fairly early on. He also soon realised that effective, relevant CRM should be at the core of his business. When we asked Simon what CRM meant to him he replied: "My view is that most businesses view customers as a one off transaction. However I believe you should look at the lifetime value of that customer. A CRM system, whatever you use, will allow you to engage that client throughout that lifetime and it will allow you to serve them better and where appropriate allow them to buy from you at a time that works for them.

For me, CRM is a system of communicating with our clients and also knowing more about our clients so we can make sure those communications are more targeted and more relevant to those people".

Although email is his preferred method of communication, Simon recognises that in this day and age, it is often an over-used tool, and businesses need to recognise that their customers must want to open their email messages: "We're actually trying to send less email out. We are making emails more targeted and so more relevant to those people, which means that when they open them, they get greater value and so they are more inclined to open them again in the future"

Other media also have a role to play. As part of his strategy to make his communication more relevant he's also increasingly using text messaging "Where possible we capture mobile phone numbers and so we can communicate by text message. I think text messaging is very powerful because it's sent to direct to someone's phone. It is likely that you get fewer texts than emails so it's more likely to be read and can be less intrusive as well because people can read it when they want. It's a great way to get information to them. We can add a call to action, and links to various websites". Simon recognises that social media also has a part to play: "I think probably Facebook works well – because so many people are on Facebook and we're having great results from that."

Simon doesn't forget the importance of face to face contact: "I think if we only did email marketing we wouldn't be so successful. Face to face contact is really important - we also use webinars a lot. Webinars let people sit at home, then go online and listen in and participate in a live broadcast."

Simon's use of CRM tools has changed overtime "When we first started, we had our own bespoke system. There was a novelty to emails back in 2003 but now they can be a bit of a pain – because people receive so many. If they get fed up they can unsubscribe, so that is why we are moving to other ways of communicating."

Simon and his team now use a sophisticated CRM tool produced by Infusionsoft. "It is a very powerful system, and what I particularly like about it, is that you can be very clever about who you communicate with, and how you communicate with them".

The system can be used to track the activity of his customers, allowing his next communication with them to be more responsive and relevant: "Say for example, I send out an email to a list of people, with a link on the email about HMOs – House of Multiple Occupancy. If they click on that link we know that they are interested in that particular topic. We can then send out more appropriate messages to the people who clicked on the link."

It means he can use what the system knows about customer interests to grow his business. Recently he launched a new Property Investors Network meeting in Wimbledon. "We were able to send a new meeting invitation email to everybody on our database who had expressed an interest in that particular part of London, and all our clients who had previously been to any other London PIN meetings. The result was a sell-out launch meeting, with 140 people registered, 110 of whom actually turned up, which for a first meeting, in a brand new venue, was a great result."

Simon's customers are not just the ones who have been to a PIN meeting or have paid for training courses. Simon recognises that his customers are on a journey. Many people first encounter his organisation by reading his book 'Property Magic', which has been on Amazon's Best Seller list since the launch of the first edition back in 2008. Having read and enjoyed the book, customers looking for more information visit the website, and then go on to register their interest in attending one of the networking meetings. "What we find is that a lot of people come to a meeting, they'll chat and meet other people who've done our training and hear about the life changing results they've achieved. Then they may come on a one-day course, and if they like that, they may come to a further advanced course. We can help people no matter where they are on their property investing journey"

As far as the future goes, Simon sees the increasing importance of high quality targeting and a multi-channel approach to customer communication; "I think we'll continue what we're doing, niching down and getting far more targeted and more specific to make sure the content is really relevant to those people, and personalise it as much as possible, which I think is really important. We need to continually make it easier for people to do business with us."

Finally Simon has three tips for anyone looking at implementing a CRM strategy: "First, think about what exactly you are looking to achieve by having a CRM system because there are lots of different systems out there. You need the one that will meet your aspirations. Secondly, pick a CRM system that is appropriate for your level of business. Infusionsoft is probably way over the top if you are just starting in business. The third is the most important. Really spend time working out what your customer wants and how to give it to them. We are always looking to provide massive value to our clients with the intention of when they come to make a buying decision, we are the go to people in the industry."

Making Your CRM Strategy Happen

"Empower your employees to make the experience great. It's good for your people because they feel confident and it's good for your customers because their problems get sorted out fast."
– Sir Richard Branson

Internal Resources – The Importance of Your People and a Senior Champion

One of the key factors contributing to the success or failure of CRM are your people. If you don't get people to buy in from the start, then your CRM strategy will most likely fail. CRM often requires your people to think, act and operate in a different way. That's why the CRM vision and objectives need to be communicated clearly throughout your company. For example, whilst your Finance team may have no involvement with your customers, they still need to understand the importance of CRM and where this will take the business. If from the outset you talk to your employees and ask them to help you define the strategy, you will be amazed how willingly and positively your employees will react. Rather than communicate the strategy downwards, develop and communicate upwards; we find that by involving people in the CRM strategy definition, they will be more supportive and enthusiastic about implementing it. Your people, especially those interacting with customers every day will know where improvements, especially on the customer experience, could be made. A great way to start is to ask your customer facing team what and where the "pain points" are and the most common customer complaints. This will give you some quick insights into where you should start looking.

Cave to Castle

However you decide to define your CRM strategy, ensure you are positive about going in this direction and try to create a real "CRM buzz" within your business. Within larger companies, put together a multi-skilled team, who will be representing their own departments - if you are a small start-up, make sure you pick the right person for this role; they need to be detail orientated, big picture watching, advocate, diplomat and visionary all rolled into one! The team will participate in customer sessions, communicate progress and ask for feedback on their ideas, proposed implementations etc. It is also important that they are good, enthusiastic communicators. Keep your team informed and communicate to them regularly about the achievements you are making; clearly communicate the direction of travel and don't forget to celebrate your successes!

The CRM vision needs to be sponsored by the Board of Directors and / or owner and they need to want it to happen as much as you do. Get them more involved - when was the last time they spoke with a customer? Get them to participate in some of the customer sessions to hear first-hand some of the issues your customers and employees are facing. Showing support from above can boost team morale enormously. In almost all cases, there is an important 'Tools' component to consider, so your CRM team need to have some experience of working with, and discussing systems.

CRM won't happen overnight, so bear in mind that your team (or CRM lead) may be committed to the project for a long period of time depending upon the complexity of the solution.

Business Processes – What Needs to Change?

What is a business process? A business process is a 'chain of events' that produce a specific outcome. It can often be visualized using a flowchart, showing the various steps. For example, consider how you currently capture information about your customers. Is it time efficient? Does it rely on different systems? Is the customer information captured in the same way across the various capture points such as through your website or Facebook page? Can you store the information in the way you want? Are you able to share this information with others in your office?

If a motivated seller fills out his details on your website, what is your follow up process? Do you have to remember to phone people back or do you have alerts reminding you when to make the next call-back? Do you have paper copies of the property details and circumstance of the seller or is the information stored electronically in one place?

For every process, map out what you are currently doing and mark out each step. Highlight the areas where improvements can be made, e.g. where you are wasting time or money. Once you have highlighted the areas for improvement, consider further tweaks to make it more beneficial.

Customer Fact
80% of CEOs believe they deliver a superior customer experience, but only 8% of their customers agree – Bain & Company

Interview – Davin Poonwassie
Keeping it Simple

As part of our series featuring some of the leading players in property, we spoke to Davin Poonwassie of Simple Backing about his property journey and discussed his views about treating customers fairly.

Davin's career up until earlier this year was in Data and Database Management, and is a Chartered IT Professional. Davin has also for many years been a contractor, advising his clients on the use and management of data both in Europe and the UK.

In addition to this, Davin has for many years been investing in property and he has a number of Buy to Let (BTL) properties. His first taste of property management was when he was at University when he Joint Ventured with his brother to buy an investment property that Davin and his friends could live in. "I have always had an interest in property from a very early age and I saw this as a good way to start investing early. And it has just got better from there. This is particularly in the last 2 years or so since I started on Kevin Green Wealth's property and mentorship coaching programme. It has opened up so much opportunity and has exposed us to many new business initiatives and ways of property investing – it has been wonderful."

Now, Davin's main focus is on Simple Backing which is a Crowdfunding and Peer to Peer Lending platform. "This is a really interesting marketplace for me as it is still fairly new in the UK. Being a property investor, I am really happy to see the finance market expanding; it provides more scope for property development and also to those who have smart business ideas."

We asked Davin what CRM meant to him: "I have been exposed to CRM for many years as a result of both my data work but also because of the CRM consultancy that my wife runs. CRM to me is about building meaningful relationships with everyone that interacts with you – whether it is your customers, prospects, suppliers, partners or anyone else. This is throughout the lifetime of that person at every stage of interaction and across every touchpoint, whether via the web, social media or by phone. With the nature of Crowdfunding, it is not possible to fund deals all of the time and so we work on building long term relationships with all of our customers – investors, borrowers and introducers."

For all of the businesses that Davin is involved with, he is an advocate of keeping it simple when it comes to tools. "For Simple Backing, we currently use a CRM system that manages all of our communications. It is from a UK based company, fairly small, and their support is great which is really important. The system is really simple to use and I can do everything I need from one place. I can set up my contact profiles, manage my diary and leads, send emails and texts, create landing pages, track and measure responses and manage all administration from one system. I have to keep an audit of all interactions that we have with our customers and prospects and this allows me to do just that.

Property management is a little different. This is currently done using many spreadsheets, filing systems and the like. This was all fine when we had a few properties but as the portfolio has increased, this takes more management. We looked in the marketplace for something that would work for us but nothing met our needs; the free stuff was either clunky or not easy to use or it simply didn't have the functionality that we needed. The high ticket priced systems were OK but they were over and above what we were looking to pay and not customer centric. So we created our own; well, what I mean by that is that we designed it and are working with a development team in the UK to create it. The 'Simple Property App' will be available soon."

We then wanted to explore Davin's views of customer and prospect communication. "For me, it is important to communicate with people when we have something relevant to say. I am not one for communicating for the sake of it as this creates time wastage on my part but also numbs our message to our customers as they would then start to regard our communication as 'noise'. Having said all that, we need to do a certain amount of interaction as this keeps us at 'front of mind' which is important for our business."

Davin then talked further about the types of communication he uses; "Our business has been systemised to an extent to ensure that our customers and prospects get consistent messaging throughout. Our brand looks consistent. Regardless of whether someone is interacting with me through social media, web, phone or face to face, our clients don't have to keep repeating themselves; everyone here who interacts with customers and prospects know exactly what has been said previously. It's like the 'McDonalds system' – you know exactly what you are getting regardless of where you are."

On the topic of communication methods, we then asked Davin what he thought were the most effective forms of communication. His response was no different to everyone else we spoke to; "The best form of communication by far is face to face. In part, this is an important step in our process for taking on borrowers and investors for the Crowdfunding business. It is a great way to get to know someone and to understand more about their goals and values. We are talking about substantial amounts of money being loaned and borrowed and we need to ensure that all of our customers know the ins and outs, including the benefits and risks, associated with being in this sector. For us, face to face is the easiest way to do this."

When asked what he feels businesses facing communication challenges should be looking at, Davin replies: "How to use social media effectively and make their communication stand out from the crowd. Social media is such a big thing now and we need to accommodate for it. I accept that some of our investors in particular may not be social media savvy at the moment but this will change. The problem is cutting through the thousands of pieces of information that is presented to a person every day. This is one of the reasons why consistency of the brand is so important to us. We also find that many people nowadays are attached to one device or another pretty much all of the time. And so the expected response times are getting shorter."

Finally, we asked Davin to give us the benefit of his experience and leave us with three tips he has found really useful when introducing CRM to his business. He replied: "Firstly, understand what you are trying to achieve from your business. Be clear about your business, your customer and prospect targets, your brand and also the service that you want to provide. Be able to explain it in simple terms as whilst you understand the ins and outs of your business, others who join after you will need to understand this in simple terms. Secondly, check-in with your customers, prospects and staff; have some sort of communication plan in place to ensure that you have a feedback mechanism – for all comments, good or bad. And thirdly, find systems and tools that work around your business and not the other way around. There are lots of businesses who start with the technology and then try to fit their business around the tools. It is like trying to fit a square peg into a round hole. There are many tools out there and something will fit with what your business is trying to achieve."

Measuring and Tracking Your CRM Success

"Statistics suggest that when customers complain, business owners and managers ought to get excited about it. The complaining customer represents a huge opportunity for more business." – Zig Ziglar

Determining the success of your CRM Strategy can be a challenging task. Based upon your business and CRM objectives, you need to decide:

1. What are the elements you are going to measure that define the success (or otherwise) of your CRM strategy? We call these Key Performance Indicators (KPIs)

2. How are you going to measure these?

3. How frequently are you going report upon these?

4. What format are you going to use for reporting?

Main Key Performance Indicators (KPIs)

Most businesses talk about KPI's. These are the main indicators they have decided to use to measure their success. The KPIs for your business are dependent upon what you have defined in your CRM strategy. For example, can an increase in sales and/or profitability solely be attributed to your CRM investment or is it due to external factors? Has your business increased overall spend per customer or do you have more customers buying smaller quantities? Are you closing more customer enquiries because your team are fast and effective or is it that the online portal that you have created for self-service is working more effectively? Once you have decided what the main KPIs are for you, monitor them regularly as part of an on-going review process. There are many KPIs your business can consider to focus on including:

1. **Sales Metrics:** enquiries, sales growth, improved sales conversion, more sales per customer, higher customer spend per order, sales per person, etc.

2. **Customer Metrics:** increase in number of new customers, quicker prospect to customer conversion times, better customer retention rates (reduced churn), improved customer satisfaction rates, fewer customer complaints, fewer returns or customer compensation given, speed of resolving customer complaints, number of referrals given etc.

3. **Marketing Measures:** improved ROI (return on investment) on marketing spend, campaign response rates, market share increase, brand awareness, media exposure, reduction in the number of unsubscribes, etc.

4. **Internal People Metrics**: improved staff morale and motivation, reduced sickness, lower staff turnover, improved efficiency, etc.

5. **Other Metrics**: reduced bad debt customers, reduced cost of service, etc.

How are you going to Measure these?

Once you have compiled a list of all the possible measurements, you need to decide which metrics you want to use for reporting. There may be complications, such as whether a metric can truly or just partly be attributed to your CRM success and whether it is easily attainable or may take too much effort or people hours to report upon. We believe it is good to define a wish list of what you want to report and based upon this list, work out what can easily be achieved in the short term, and what requires more effort for the medium and longer terms. It could be that some metrics are not possible to achieve today as you don't have the data to support it. By creating a wish list of reporting, you can then start to collect any data that may be missing from now.

When you have defined your metrics, you will need to set a base line (understanding where the business is today which will then be used as a marker to show improvement or change) for each metric against which you can measure your progress. Don't worry if you don't have a base line, as it doesn't take long to build up a history to see progress within your business. It could be that your base line for managing customer enquiries is as simple as 'I only follow up on 10% of the enquiries that I receive through my website' or I have 20% churn year on year in my business (where customers leave your business).

Reporting Frequency

The frequency of reporting very much depends upon your business. Do you have a business where people are purchasing products daily, weekly, monthly or may be only once per year or even longer? Think for example of a supermarket versus a car dealer or an estate agent. All of these businesses will have completely different metrics and reporting frequencies.

Most businesses will require a weekly and monthly metric, with sales reports required weekly and customer service reports required monthly. If you are a lettings managing agent for example, your reporting may be daily or weekly depending upon the number of rental payments that you manage.

Reporting Format

We very much believe in using visual metrics for reporting. Often companies produce complex reports with lots of numbers. In this case we would suggest producing a one page executive summary with an overview of the most important measures with some detail behind it. This means that your team can look at a metric at top level and then see further detail related to his/her area of responsibility. Your team will be looking at different elements of reporting, e.g. the Sales team will want to look at sales conversions whereas the Customer Services team wants to look at the resolution timescales of complaints.

With reporting also comes the question about access rights i.e. who can view certain information. Every business is different, but our view is that transparency is key. It can be a great motivator for staff if certain KPI's are not met, highlighting areas for improvement and working towards resolving these.

Nowadays, there are many tools that provide standard reports and it is up to the business to decide which of these they would like to use for reporting. Again reports will develop over time and look for a solution which is easy to use, easily adapted and easily integrated with your IT infrastructure.

Something About Customer Metrics

It is very important to start monitoring customer metrics, as CRM is very much about the customer. However, customer metrics often involve talking to or researching customer behaviour, hence not something you will want to do on a daily or weekly basis. However, as a quick win, you may wish to consider something like the following:

Customer Feedback Faces ('Customer Smileys')

This technique is a quick way to measure customer satisfaction and can be used at different customer touch points or interactions. It asks customers to indicate whether they are happy (green / left smiley), indifferent (orange / middle smiley) or unhappy (red / right smiley). It is very easy for the customer to click on and doesn't take a lot of effort. Always provide the opportunity for customers to elaborate on their response. The question can be emailed to customers, with a reminder follow up for non-responders.

Customer feedback faces are good for providing a quick overview of customer satisfaction at any point in time. For example, service smileys below:

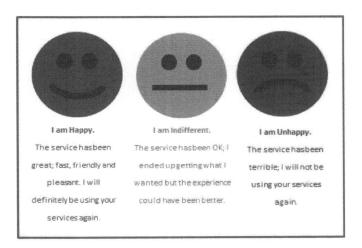

Customer Fact

Emails with social sharing buttons increase click-through rates by 158% - Social Fresh. Articles with images get 94% more views than those without – NewsCred.

Interview – John Lee and Vincent Wong
The Importance of Customer Targeting

John Lee and Vincent Wong founded Wealth Dragons in 2009, a business which is now one of the UK's most successful organisers of Property Investment coaching and events, and between them they've helped thousands of people achieve their property goals. We spent some time with them recently talking about their background in property, and their views on CRM and how it's driving their business.

Vincent was born in Liverpool 1969. He went to the London University become a pharmacist, but already knew that wasn't what wanted to do ultimately - "Inside of me I always felt that I was a business entrepreneur. Then I didn't think much about it until I went to university and graduated in pharmacy. And then I really started to get bored".

An ex-girlfriend had given him a copy of Unleash the Power Within by the well-known motivational speaker and author Anthony Robbins. It stayed on his shelf until the relationship broke down and he decided he needed to think about his future: "Then I picked up this book that had gathered dust for the last year and a half and read it from cover to cover." Inspired, he decided on a change of career, and studied for a MBA, expecting that it would get him access to a highly paid job in banking or consultancy. He was to be disappointed, "After getting the MBA, I did not get the job that I wanted. I was offered something that was so entry level it wouldn't even pay my mortgage."

A further venture failed in the dot.com crash, but at the time he had bought a flat in Clapham and sold it a year later for a healthy profit; "I realised that if I had actually taken the money that I had raised for my business and put it in property I would have been very successful. I decided then and there that property's got to be my game."

John Lee was born in Burnley, Lancashire in 1981. After graduating from Hull University he started working in the animation industry but at the age of 21 he made the decision to get out of the rat race and build a property-based business. John had become a big believer in the value of professional coaching, so for him the first step was obvious; "Most people know the story about when I sold my car and I paid a guy 10 grand to coach me. One of the early lessons I learned is you pay for the best advice that you can afford, and so that's what I could afford at the time". Even now, as the owner of a successful business, John remains an advocate of the value of the best advice; "I still have coaches in everything I do. So that's how I got started in business".

Our first question was to ask what the term 'Customer' meant to John and Vincent. John's reply was revealing: "We don't see them as customers, we see them as clients. There's a big distinction; the first are transactional, but clients are someone you help - you have their best interests at heart and you do whatever it takes to get that person what they need". He goes on: "I always used to wonder why businesses focus on making just one sale. It's something you often see; they make the one sale and they never contact the client again - they never add value. For us it's all about adding value".

They take a similar strategic view about prospects; "A prospect is someone who is a potential client – but only if they meet our criteria. Let me say that again, if they meet our criteria. Not all clients are good for your business!" This is a sentiment that we totally understand and agree with – the best clients aren't always the ones who have the biggest billings. Vincent explains the Wealth Dragon's approach to understanding their different customer types: "We think all business should segment their client base. We grade our clients from A to E. 'A' clients are people who buy from you, they love what you do and they're grateful for amazing results they get. The B and C clients are a little bit more demanding in terms of our time. You have to work quite hard to satisfy them - and quite rightly so! If they're going to spend money, then they should get their money's worth. The D clients are much more time consuming to service, and E clients are just not worth your while, in fact the E clients cost you money in the long run. We concentrate on looking after our A, B, C clients and do not actively focus on our D & E client as much".

He goes on to talk about the CRM system Wealth Dragons use, and how they leverage it to build great relationships with their customers; "For many clients, we know the major events that happen to them – because they're happy to share that information. So we can send a congratulations note or sometimes even flowers - to recognise a birthday, or anniversary, or even the arrival of a new baby. Again it all comes back to not seeing them as a 'customer' but as a client and as a friend".

This strategy hasn't always been in place and it comes from learning from mistakes John and Vincent have made in the past: "We never really used to pay attention to our existing clients. I think it's one of the cardinal sins that we commit ourselves. Now we recognize our clients, our A, B clients are just so important. We go out of our way to reach out to them rather than just wait for them to knock on our door".

The CRM system they use to support their strategy is InfusionSoft, a US marketing automation system aimed at small and medium sized businesses.

John is a big fan of the system and its ability to score leads and make follow up marketing activity easy: "The system's ability for resends is so quick to use – just a few clicks using the Campaign Builder tool. So if I set up an email to go to 100,000 people, I can also easily set up another email to just those who haven't opened the first one – boom! We've also set up a lead scoring system, so if for example someone enters my list in the first month, we're not going to send them marketing emails to buy things because I know they're not ready. Our points system runs from between 0 and 1,000, 1,000 means you're ready to take it to the next level and 0 means you're not ready."

John continues: "I also really like the InfusionSoft app called Snap. When I go to networking events, I am given thousands of business cards. Most people don't do much with the cards they collect - they literally have all the wealth in these cards stuck in the drawer of the desk. But after each event I line up all the business cards, take a picture of them, and the details automatically get loaded into the CRM system!"

The system can be used to tag the individual: "Say I meet someone who's interested in speaking at one of our events. I can tag this person interested in speaking and we will automatically fire off a sequence of communications. Like -

"Hey John, great meeting you at the event. How's things? By the way we spoke about public speaking. I think it's a really good tip for you check this out!" This technology does come with a learning curve; "When it first came out, it was very complicated to use and now it's much easier. Now if I can't find a tab or contact, Infusionsoft's customer service team are there to help! They send you a video which tells you exactly where it is. Their customer service is the best I've ever experienced".

The CRM system really provides the Wealth Dragons with insight they couldn't gain any other way: "We know that for marketing, it used to be seven communications before people took action. It is now 30. So when we send one email out we only get a 10% open rate. They write another email, send it to the same people again, and you guess what you get a 5% open rate, the seventh email you send it again you get a 2% open rate.

However, in John's view having a strategic plan in marketing or CRM is nothing without the marketing systems to execute it. "Great strategies are good for your boss if that's what they require but it doesn't work without a way to make it happen. The reason why we use the Infusionsoft CRM system religiously, and why we rave about it so much, is that it's got the CRM and amazing marketing tools together".

We asked John and Vincent what they thought were the coming trends in client or customer management. John replied "I think client service will be a lot more personal. Often I'm on a call with someone and I'll realise that we're just not connecting. I'm just adding massive value and they'll come back and say hey John can you come and coach me? I ask why I should coach them. I really love to do this so if I think they're serious I'll take them on."

There's still a lot of ambition left at the Wealth Dragons! When we asked Vince about the future of the business he replied: "We want to become a household name - we want people to think of the Wealth Dragons as the first port of call if they want to change their lives. Right now, talking about wealth is still a bit of a taboo - I want to popularise it so that wealth creation, making money on top of your job, is acceptable and we can help them. And I want Wealth Dragons to be a trusted brand a bit like Virgin. Even though Richard Branson is not really involved in a lot of the Virgin products and services but it's still something that signifies quality and value for money. So I want to build us into a strong brand that people can identify with. That's it really!"

Finally we asked Vince and John for some final thoughts on the importance of CRM for modern businesses. Vince replied: "I think Customer Relationship Management and lead generation is fundamentally important but still an underutilised aspect of business. A message needs to go out for people to learn it and master the basic skills". John added: If businesses want to get to a big level, they need to invest the time and money to learn the CRM stuff. If they don't then they are not going to change anything. If I was to give a growing business advice it would be "You need to become the best marketer you can be, you need to learn everything there is to know about sales and you need a CRM system. That's what you need. And the things that glues it together is pay for the best advice you can afford!"

Interview - Keith Penny

The Importance of Using Correct Customer Communications

We met with Keith Penny of Pennymatters to talk about the strategies he uses for effectively communicating with his customers.

In the difficult market of the last few years, Pennymatters has established itself as one of the leading financial advice companies in the South East, offering a full range of financial products and advice to a growing client base. As well as working with a number of estate agents in the area, Pennymatters are now finding more and more of their customers are property investors with substantial property portfolios. In order to accommodate for this, Pennymatters has a number of specialist advisors that are able to provide the best mortgage advice for clients in that position.

After a background studying in accountancy and then starting a career in advising in financial services, Keith set up Pennymatters around five years ago. When we asked him what he enjoys most about his role he replies: "I love seeing my clients benefit from the good financial advice provided over the years. I've had clients able to claim when their relative has died or suffered illnesses, and I've had loads of clients retire happily with planning that I've set up. It's good to see them reap the rewards from advice I provided. Also having a business which other advisers want to operate through means that I can indirectly help more clients."

Keith is clear on definitions of his customers and prospects: "A customer is someone that we've engaged with - primarily someone that has physically either paid for our services or taken up some advice that has generated a financial reward for us, whereas a prospect is someone that we're starting to engage with who hasn't yet physically signed our terms of business".

When it comes to long term relationships with customers, Keith is able to identify two groups, each with their own needs; "We have two types of clients – the first type are mortgage and protection clients and are transactional so they come to us when they want either to buy or re-mortgage a house or arrange or review some protection. We don't really have to service that client; once somebody's bought a house or started a life insurance policy then generally we can't add value to the relationship by calling them every year. The second type of client is where we manage their investment, savings, or pension plans. That isn't transactional so we have a 3 tiered proposition that's designed to deliver the appropriate two-way communication. For the lowest tier, the client will get a 3-year review, whereas clients in our highest tier are entitled to a quarterly review. And of course all clients can call us as they need to." Keith recognises that not all clients are the same; "Some clients you ring once a year and they don't want to see us because they are happy - they'll say they will call us when they need us. But they're happy with that two way process– if we need them, we'll call them and if they need us, they can call us."

Pennymatters use a CRM System to trigger those reviews, allowing Keith's team to do their preparation in advance of the scheduled client meeting, manage the appointment, and handle any follow-up activity. They also look for key milestones in a client's life: "Each month I look for clients who are about to celebrate a big birthday - the ones with a zero; 30, 40, 50 or 60s! We send the client a card and then make sure our advisor follows that up; I personally feel little things like that make a big difference."

When it comes to the best way to communicate with his clients Keith is clear: "Face to face is best because you can look them in the eye, you can understand them, see their body language, ask proper questions and get the right answers. Saying that, it's difficult to do face to face all the time so after that I'll telephone - because when you hear a voice it means something. Email is a poor third, most clients get so many it just diminishes the importance".

However, Keith is happy to use email where customers prefer; "We provide personalised portals for our clients letting them access valuations of their investments and pensions 24/7 on a smart phone or a tablet. They can use it to communicate with us but some clients find it a lot easier to send us a quick email, rather than log into their website and send a message."

He feels developments in this area are going to continue, as his business tries to increase the number of clients their advisors can effectively service; "A few clients now like to speak to us via Skype and I expect the use of video conversations will grow so that clients will just have to press one button on their computer or smartphone and a video pops up and I will be able to talk to them in their office."

We asked Keith for his final thoughts on the subject of effective communication with customers and he replied: "For me it's all about simplicity, you just want something that is simple, that works, which makes sure you're doing what you say you will do. Sometimes I feel we over-do what we think our clients want and end up doing lots of stuff that they actually don't value. Asking clients for feedback is something we plan to start doing better, so that we understand what they actually want, and we don't waste our time doing all this fancy stuff that and in reality isn't valued by our customers. This shall help us to keep our fees keen, and not simply to try and justify a higher charge'.

The Importance of Data

"Data is a precious thing and will last longer than the systems themselves." – Tim Berners-Lee

There's no getting away from this; its data that drives modern business, and more importantly for us; underpins most CRM strategies. Luckily, as an entrepreneur or property business person you don't have to be an IT whizz to manage a very effective CRM strategy, but anyone who is serious about their business will have to be familiar with the compliance aspects of collecting customer and prospect data, and some basic good practises around gathering, using and storing data. Data churns at approximately 20% per year. This means that 20% of the information you have in your customer / prospect database will no longer be valid after 12 months.

The content provided in this section is correct as of the time of writing. However, the data protection regulations are likely to change often due to the methods of easy data capture and the increase in online communications. In order to check for updates, please visit www.ico.org.uk.

Data Protection and Electronic Communication – The Rules

This is very important for all business so we thought we'd spend a bit of time on it now. Get Data Protection wrong and you can find yourself in real trouble, but follow some common sense guidelines and the principles can work to your advantage.

The increase in computerisation in the 1980s and 1990s brought with it considerable concerns about what customer data was being collected, and how it

---

was being used. More recently, the way data was being used by some businesses for email and telephone marketing started to worry and even irritate consumers.

The result was the introduction of legislation defining the responsibilities of businesses in respect to the care and use of their customer's data. In the EU, a broad framework was agreed, leaving national governments some latitude, but essentially similar legislation around the security and use of data is now in place in every one of the 28 EU countries. As a result, misuse of customer data can have severe consequences, including, in extreme cases, very large fines and even prison sentences.

The UK's response was to pass Acts of Parliament that affects all organisations holding data on individuals in the UK - even small businesses and voluntary organisations.

It's potentially a complex area, and in here we'll aim to cover the main points you'll need to consider when putting together a CRM strategy, and help you identify potential danger areas.

First and foremost, if you are keeping or using any personal data on your customer you'll need to register with the Information Commissioner's Office (ICO). 'Personal data' includes names and addresses, email addresses, phone numbers and so on – and it includes people in their private and business capacities. The process is quite straightforward, although there's a small fee to pay and registration needs to be renewed each year. The ICO's website is www.ico.org.uk and you can use the site to register electronically. Incidentally, there is a lot more information on the usage of data here and we strongly suggest that you take a look.

You also need to keep the data secure. For most organisations that means implementing common-sense standard business practise – using firewalls, passwords, not leaving laptops or USB sticks on the train, keeping back-ups and not using un-coded email attachments to transfer data. A simple trap many fall into is to use 'CC' when sending an email, so all recipients can see all the addresses. If you're using standard email software for marketing make sure you use the 'BCC' function. Also, if you send data by email, it is often advisable to ensure it is password protected (and do not include the password in the same communication).

There's an additional class of data that's known as 'Sensitive'. It includes things like racial origins, health information, political views, sexual orientation, financial details or details of legal proceedings. This may well include data you hold on tenants, so quite reasonably if you're keeping data of this nature you have to be even more conscious of the need for security.

All your customers now have a right to know what data you're keeping on them. If they send a 'Subject Access Request' you have to send them a copy of any data you store within a reasonable period of time; so make sure you know where it is, and prepare a standard report that can be run on demand. If any of the information you have is wrong you'll need to be prepared to update it, and if asked, delete it.

When building up your customer databases only ask for the information that's reasonably needed for you to run your customer's business effectively – you're are not allowed to collect data you don't need, so stick to asking for information you will actually use. And don't keep it any longer than necessary, plan on reviewing your data systems every year and archive or remove old data. By 'old' we usually mean more than 48 months, unless there's a compliance case for keeping it longer.

Outside The UK

Sending personal data on residents of Europe out of the EU area is problematic, as European authorities regard protection provided for data outside of the 32 EU & EEA countries (i.e. Switzerland, Norway, Iceland and Lichtenstein) as inadequate. So be careful if you are, for example, using an outsourcing supplier on the Indian subcontinent or there's any danger your suppliers are outsourcing.

If you need to send data to the US, there is a certification process meeting EU standards that American organisations can use. It's called 'Safe Harbor', and you can find more details at: **http://export.gov/safeharbor/index.asp.** Again, the authorities in EU countries will hold you responsible if personal data you are holding or using ends up in an unprotected foreign system.

The rules around usage of data for email and phone are slightly different in Europe compared to the UK. That's down to the way each nation implemented the original EU framework. For example, in the UK, you're free to email and phone individuals at businesses (except partnerships and sole traders) without receiving their permission. This isn't the case in most other EU countries. Similarly, you can also contact all your old and existing customers about other goods and services you offer without specific permission – not necessarily the case in other EU states.

Using Data for Marketing

When it comes to collecting and using data for sending out marketing messages, there are some guidelines you should keep to. Most are the practises you'll commonly see being used by the well-known organisations you'll encounter every day; ask for permission before you collect email addresses or phone numbers for marketing give customers the opportunity to 'opt-out' each time you contact them and make it clear who you are and why you are communicating with them when you email or phone.

As you can see above, while there's a little more latitude in the UK when it comes to using personal data for marketing, this isn't the case in every EU country. We'd suggest that it's better, both from a compliance and customer service point of view, to cover all the bases when it comes to asking customers and prospects for their information; specify why you're asking, what you're using it for – and also make it clear whether you will be sharing it with other organisations. This is the sort of reassurance consumers are now beginning to expect from any reputable company. If you state that you are not going to share your data with 3rd parties, it is still possible to send your customer base marketing activity on behalf of another company as long as you do not release the data.

If you're using 'cold lists' that you've bought or rented for marketing (a list of contacts where the people on that list are not aware of you or the products / services that you provide), you are responsible for checking with the list owner that those on the list have given their permission. You'll then have to get them checked against suppression lists held by any reputable agency (a list of people who have in effect opted-out of marketing), and also make sure anyone who has told you they no longer want to hear from you is removed from the list. Any good CRM or email marketing system will help you manage this.

If you have a website that uses cookies don't forget you have to offer the customers the opportunity to accept them.

This is just a brief summary of the key points you'll need to bear in mind as you construct a CRM strategy. There's more on the ICO website, www.ico.org.uk/for_organisations.

Customer Fact
The total amount of data being captured and stored by industry doubles every 1.2 years – Source

Interview – Juswant and Sylvia Rai
Providing Consistent Customer Experiences

It was great to meet Sylvia and Juswant Rai of Berkshire Property Meet (BPM) to talk about their careers in property as well as how a focus on customers and a personal touch has contributed towards their building a business that has attracted over 18,000 delegates to their events in the past 8 years.

Before starting BPM, both were in full time jobs with big companies, Juswant in IT, while Sylvia was a FTSE 100 accountant.   They both already had an interest in property, but it was the influence of a book that kicked off a life changing decision to start their own business - Rich Dad Poor Dad by Robert Kiyosaki. It inspired them to start planning an exit strategy from the corporate world.

Looking around, it became obvious to them both that the property market could have potential for them - they were both interested, and it was at the time when building a BTL portfolio was starting to become an accepted option to a 'normal' career.

Not knowing where to start, Juswant searched the web and discovered a regular property networking event was taking place just around the corner from his workplace. After going a few times, he discovered that talking to people who already had experience in the industry was much more valuable than trying to teach himself, and both he and Sylvia became regular attendees at similar events across the country.

They quickly discovered that that there were no similar networking events near where they lived in the Thames Valley, and decided they could try to set one up themselves, and BPM was born, initially no more than asking the Facebook property group they belonged to if anyone wanted to meet up at a local pub.

Sylvia and Juswant rapidly discovered that offering like-minded people the opportunity to come along to a venue one evening a month, spend an hour talking to each other and then listen to an expert was a winning formula and the Berkshire Property Meet is a now a well-established and successful forum in the industry.

They have very clear ideas about the sort of culture they want at BPM and they work hard at creating a supportive environment at their events. "People say it's friendly and it's very helpful but it didn't just happen. It's something we encourage." They also stick to the same well proven format "It's a bit like McDonalds! People know what to expect when they come to one of our events, so messing around just because we (the organisers) get bored of the format doesn't reflect the needs of our attendees". However, they don't lose sight of the real reason their customers attend: "It's about business and it's about money. People are there because they want to do business and it's important this fact is not lost. It is very serious. "

At the same time as establishing BPM, Sylvia and Juswant took their own first steps into the property market. They realised property was a people business as much as it was about bricks and mortar, and when we asked what they enjoyed most about their business, the reply wasn't unexpected; "As clichéd as it sounds, it's the people! We have a lot of tenants, we have the estate agents that we deal with, we have all the different personal aspects of running our own portfolio, and there are the people we meet through BPM. All our businesses begin and end with the people involved."

When they were starting to build up their own business, the market, especially in the Midlands where they decided to focus, was very hot. They were learning all the time, and were also able to start putting together packages of properties for other investors.

Not long after this the 2007/8 economic crash arrived and Sylvia and Juswant expected the market (and the BPM) to be badly affected. However their business unexpectedly boomed - they discovered people wanted somewhere secure to put their money and protect their wealth, and were looking to property. The demand for networking events accelerated and suddenly they were running two or three events a month. "I think it was partly because people were looking for a sense of security. They enjoyed networking with other property investors; "What are you doing? How are you doing it?", and the best thing was people came along to help each other out. It was the complete opposite to what we thought would happen."

Sylvia and Juswant have a simple philosophy when it comes to their customers: "We treat them the same way we would want to be treated!" It's also great for us to hear them talking about CRM without any mention of IT! "Customer Relationship

Management for us is looking after the people whether they are tenants or attendees. We know that a tenant in a room for six months has a certain value. But if we look after them for let's say twelve months, the value increases exponentially. If they stay for longer, it grows because every time a tenant comes and goes, there is a cost - not just monetary, but time. So looking after them and making sure that they are happy when they are there and the value of that customer grows massively."

They take the same approach to prospects: "Customer acquisition may take a long time, but we build relationships with prospects in the same way. I know in the marketing world its accepted that people need to have seven touches or seven connections or seven reassurances or seven recognitions or whatever they want to call it before they actually will feel comfortable with either contacting or purchasing, and our 'brand' is designed to support that relationship. We have deliberately not hidden behind a logo and we deliberately don't have a corporate brand. We branded our business as us because it is part of the relationship we build with our customers; "This is us, this is who we are, we have nothing to hide, come and meet us"."

The same people orientated philosophy also benefits their rental business: "We get tons of leads from people who have told their friends about the houses we have – usually because they are better than some of the ones their friends are living in or offer much better value".

That desire for a personal touch means they prefer conversations to email, Juswant says: "If somebody sends us a text or an email or puts something up on Facebook where the message could be mis-construed, the first thing I do is write straight back to them and say, "Here is my contact number, give me a call". It is so easy to misinterpret their email or text and then your response is misread and that quickly escalates completely out of our control because you are not hearing their voice, you are not seeing their eyes, you are not understanding the feeling behind when they wrote it. So I just say, "Pick up the phone".

Inevitably, because of the numbers of customers they have, BPM do use some marketing tools: "Because so many people are interested in attending we use AWeber to help manage our customer relationships. The reason why we chose that system is because everybody else emailing us was using AWeber and if it is good enough for them then it is also good enough for us! It is a very simple system. We have looked at other systems that are more complex, but then the cost grows exponentially. At the minute, AWeber gives us what we need. If we were then to try change what we're doing then we might need to look at other systems. But right now it gives us 99.99999% delivery".

BPM are very focussed on getting the frequency of their communications right – although they accept that what's ok for some customers isn't right for all: "Most people look forward to our emails, although some people don't. But they know that what they are going to receive is consistent. Sometimes they'll love reading it, and hopefully they'll get at least one pearl of wisdom each time. Sometimes they don't have the time and it gets deleted. That's absolutely fine. They can choose to unsubscribe".

Often their marketing uses short videos, usually 2-3 minutes long, featuring the next speaker. Campaigns for each event follow a similar pattern: "We start from the moment the last BPM finished, and from then till the next event, it's all about promoting the event using a mix of media: social media, photos, videos, email".

We were also interested to hear that BPM have never used a rented or bought in list of names in their marketing: "Everybody's opted in to our list. Some people just gave us their business cards, but everybody on our list has asked to be on it.

They've all opted in and they can just as easily opt out. It's just one click to opt in and one click to opt out."

BPM used social media from an early stage "A lot of people I knew were getting on Facebook, but Twitter didn't even exist then. YouTube was about but we did not really use it. We used Facebook to build credibility: we were saying that we got 150 people in, so let's stick some photographs that show those people in the room. We are not just saying it - this is social proof."

Nowadays Facebook is still probably the biggest tool they use; Juswant comments: "People interact with us on our Facebook page and our group and through other Facebook property groups. But I still don't really understand Twitter! Even though I've got an account it still doesn't make sense to me, although I know some people one day will work it out. YouTube is also great, it's the biggest search engine after Google, and our videos get hundreds of hits.

We'll leave the final word to Sylvia: "Treat customers how you would like to be treated - I think that this is really important. But don't let the customer control you because then you will lose your own focus and direction. By all means listen, but the balance has to be right - you don't want the tail wagging the dog. There needs to be an equal partnership, with respect on both sides. Be aligned with your values, run your business with integrity and don't focus on the money. The money will come. Focus on the relationships, because if you get that right, the business will work."

Interview – Daniel Latto

Adding Value to Customer Communications

Recently, we had the privilege of meeting business and property coach Dan Latto, and asked him about his background in property and how he uses CRM to manage and grow his business.

Like many property entrepreneurs, Dan started on a more conventional career path: "I always remember wanting to work for myself. I left university after six months because I really didn't enjoy it and I went into the world of work. It didn't take me long to realise how rubbish that was too! I hated working for someone else; working for a boss who thought he knew better and wouldn't listen to a good idea. But I really tried to learn everything I could from that period; I took on everything. I was the first to get there, the last to leave. I also started investing in property. Those really were the golden years, right at the start of the property boom, and it was very easy to make money. I bought, sold, and renovated properties and was able to build up a portfolio large enough to allow me to retire just before I turned 30."

Later, Dan started to get more involved in business coaching; "In that time I built up a lot of experience, not only in property but in business generally, so that's what I do now. I have a coaching business that aims to take a person from point A to point B quicker than they would get there if they did it themselves."

When we asked Dan what he enjoys most about coaching, he replied "A couple of things, really. The first thing is helping people get results; being able to take someone who actually cannot see the light at the end of the tunnel from that negative place, and bringing them to a place where they can achieve anything they want to".

We then asked Dan to talk about his customers a little more: "I don't really like to use the word 'customer' - I don't see them as being customers; I see them more like friends. Certainly at the start of our relationship they're a client but as we move on, we get to understand each other, and that relationship develops too." It's an interesting point – the relationship built between a coach and their client clearly has a lot in common with what we'd normally think of as a friendship.

But clearly when Dan first meets his clients they're a prospect: "I think of a prospect as someone who is aware of you. You've got an email address or they've subscribed to your YouTube channel or maybe you've got their home address but they're someone who has expressed an interest in what I do. I don't think of prospects as a random person that you have sent a letter to hoping they'll respond - but those who have in some way requested communication from you. There are really two main types of people we aim for; property and business. But there is a third type of person that's more difficult to clearly define and this is someone who is disappointed at where they are in life - they recognise that they want more but they're not quite sure how to move forward. "

Moving on, we asked Dan about the role CRM plays in modern businesses: "At it's most basic level, it's email marketing and that's what most small businesses think of when you talk about CRM. Then there's more complex stuff, still with email, but sending newsletters and keeping regular contact with clients and prospects. They could be using a tool like AWeber, MailChimp or Constant Contact. At the next level, businesses will be segmenting customers - so if you send out a hundred emails and half opened their email, you can send them a follow-up email depending if they opened it or not. A tool like Infusionsoft would probably fit into that category. A stage beyond that is usually for much bigger businesses when they need information like names, addresses, product purchase history which they can again segment".

When we asked Dan about the CRM system his own business uses he replied: "About five years ago I started off with Constant Contact, but then I moved to using AWeber because it had more functionality for what I needed. I tested Infusionsoft but it was too complex for us at that stage. I used AWeber and that worked really well for me - it's cost effective and easy to set up and use. But it's a little clunky, and sometime a little bit slow because it's a Software as a Service application (also known as SaaS) so the response time is dependent on your internet connection. I have outgrown AWeber and recently transitioned to Active Campaign as this does both CRM and email marketing in an all in one solution".

Dan is a believer that robust business processes are as important as CRM tools when it comes to building successful relationships with customers and prospects; "I managed 250 properties for my letting agency using Excel. We systemised it and it worked perfectly so we grew our business without needing third party software - until we got to a stage where the business size meant it became unusable. It showed the importance of process; we had a step by step strategy for bringing customers on board and then how we managed that customer and added additional value. You start by drawing customer flow diagrams showing where this customer goes, when they buy our product, and what else can be done to give them additional value".

The response that we got from Dan when we asked him to suggest some other businesses that in his experience implement CRM effectively was an interesting one; "I must admit, I do find it difficult because as soon as you said, 'Do I recall any companies that do CRM really well?' what immediately springs to mind are the big businesses who do it incredibly badly! It seems to me that the companies that are able to spend money on CRM either have untrained staff working for them or they just don't know how to do it! One company that's slightly different is Apple. I'm not a huge Apple fan but I'm an Apple user and when I've had any problems with my products, the customer service genuinely has been very good".

On the topic of social media, we asked Dan which platforms worked best for him: "Facebook undoubtedly works best. Twitter drives traffic but it doesn't create conversations. People might then subscribe but really conversations happen in two places, one is on Facebook and the second one is our website where we've got Facebook plug-ins. We also use a private Facebook group where you get to meet other people who are in a similar journey as you".

Facebook and Twitter aren't the only platforms Dan uses to deliver marketing content; "We use different channels to get to different people and so far, alongside Facebook and Twitter, we have a digital magazine, use YouTube for videos and also have a 'Property Coaching & Wealth Creation' podcast that you can download from iTunes. It's designed to position us as an expert in the field for growing businesses - people can download it on to their iPad or tablet and it works very well. We also do webinars before an event so that when they get to the event people will know what I sound like, what I look like and what the story is. We find they're very effective in breaking down boundaries and even before the event starts we've started to create trust between me and the prospect". All in all, Dan believes in using multiple channels to reach out to help people who may otherwise be stuck.

Dan also finds webinars an effective way to deliver content and value to clients. "I hold a webinar once every two weeks and make them very interactive and engaging. I try to make them funny because that retains people's attention span, I put jokes in there and put stories in there. Quite a few people have said that the best bit is listening to all the success stories because it's really motivational. It's like being at a live event where people often go off sharing their experiences and then tell the next person, 'That was amazing, I felt this, I felt that was great!' While I like videos, there is no interactivity – it's only me talking to a camera whereas while on the webinar I can see feedback".

We're all great believers in the importance of measuring the effectiveness of any investment in marketing. So we asked Dan how he measured his marketing campaigns: "We keep a close eye on various key performance indicators, and we know we're getting about a 35% open-rate which is very good. We compare various email subject lines - they are key in determining whether our email will get opened. So we look at what the open rate is and then we'll change the subject line - sometimes we'll try testing different ones through social media as well."

Trying to keep those open-rates up is an ongoing challenge for Dan: "Generally speaking open-rates on business emails are dropping dramatically; you've got to focus on adding value every time. When someone subscribes to your email, you can't just send any kind of a poor quality email. First of all it's got to be relevant, it's got to be interesting and it's got to have value otherwise they'll **unsubscribe** because all customers and prospects are just a single button away from **un**subscribing!".

That's not the only challenge Dan has faced over the years, he's also had to innovate and change his strategy as the market and his business developed: "We used to send emails out once a month but once a month isn't just enough anymore. We all get subjected to something like 3,000 marketing messages a day and one email amongst those is just going to get deleted and lost. Now when I send an email out, people will click and listen, knowing that next week, there's another one coming. We're also beginning to collect addresses so that we can send postcards once a quarter. The post card will just have different messaging, like the latest copy of the magazine, go and watch all these videos, there's a live event coming up and so on. It means we're using multiple channels; video, digital magazine, social media, email and now actual post cards that go to your letter box!"

Wanting to explore the innovation theme further, we asked Dan what he sees as the coming trends in customer management. "I see businesses moving away from delivering the same to everyone to more specific segmentation and almost towards a one on one relationship. Have you seen Jerry Maguire? Jerry said 'The key is not more clients; the key is fewer clients and great retention'. Everything is also getting faster, many big organisations are like dinosaurs - it takes years to make a decision and by the time they've made their decision, it's too late! So I see more mid-range companies coming up and competing with the big boys. They're not too small like say, a single shop, but big enough to matter, yet they're still able to change rapidly to meet their customer's changing demands. They can do this by empowering their staff – especially the ones that deal direct with customers. Recently I had with a problem with a utility bill and they said, 'Right, we'll send you a new bill next month.' So I waited a month, a new bill came and there was a late payment charge of £6. I was thinking, 'You told me to wait and then you charge me because I followed what you said?' What they should've allowed their staff to do instead is to say 'We're so sorry about that, we'll waive that £6 and then we'll sort it out'".

Finally we asked Dan what tips he would offer anyone thinking of introducing CRM into his or her business. "They've got to understand what CRM is going to be used for first. A mistake businesses often make is that they think that they should have a CRM system, but they don't know what it is and they don't know what it should be doing. But they still buy one, spend lots of money and time setting it up, then hardly anyone uses it. Imagine I have some bricks and I start building a house and I've got no plan - I just start laying some bricks and cement. Well it will be a nightmare house. I see so many people building their business, their relationships, their health and their CRM systems without any firm ideas or blueprint, and I say that is the fast-track to failure for CRM or anything else. People should have a clear idea what it is that they want from implementing CRM before doing anything. Some people might say, 'Well, it's more sales, isn't it?' Well, it might be but how are you going to do that? What is the actual process, what is the value proposition that you are going to give that will allow you to do that? All this needs to be properly figured out before you start spending money on the technology!"

One of the things we've learnt through the various interviews is that there are many different approaches to growing a sustainable business by building effective relationships with your customers. Dan proves there's still room for innovation in how this is achieved.

The Importance of Data (Continued)

"The goal is to turn data into information, and information into insight." – Carly Fiorina

Adding Value / Permission Based Marketing

As we've mentioned above, processing, storing and analysing customer information is being made more restrictive through legislation as governments respond to public concerns about privacy and the use of their data by organisations. Then again by being aware and working within the spirit as well as the rules of the law, companies can gain greater value from their customer data. It's called Permission Marketing, and it involves you making a deal with your customers and prospects; you give us your data and we'll give you a more personal and more relevant customer experience. It is therefore key to ensure you get permission from your customers and prospects to use their data to service their needs and enquiries demonstrably better. If you deal with this in a respectable way, most consumers will have no hesitation to allow you to use their data. In our experience businesses usually discover permission based marketing is a more effective way of generating high quality responses and building sales.

Preferred Channels of Communication

When gathering permission from customers don't forget to also ask them to suggest their preferred way for you to communicate with them, and even how often they would like to hear from you, and at what time of the day. A lot of customers now object to telephone marketing, especially via mobile phones (still considered very intrusive) and surprisingly large numbers still prefer a well-addressed direct mail letter or email.

Also take into consideration the age of your customer audience. Whilst mobile phone penetration is high, not all customers use data or even text services, especially older consumers, while even within the younger generations, some youngsters resist the newer forms of technology. Keep this information up to date and let customers easily change and modify their permission settings. Capturing and utilising preferred channels of communication increases the efficiency of marketing communications and reduces wastage. Not only therefore will it help you in being more effective in dealing with your customers, but the respect it shows gains their respect and trust in dealing with your business in the future.

Data Hygiene – The Importance of Keeping Your Data Clean

To make the most out of your CRM environment, the data and the information contained in your database must be accurate - remember the old saying "garbage in, garbage out"? Here are the main things to consider:

1. What information are you going to capture? When collecting data consider what information you would like to collect and for what purpose. For example, data from a survey may be relevant today, but it may get out of date really quickly.

2. Decide on the rules about what information is captured and stick to it. For example, if you have a first name field, do not enter anything but the first name in that field. A first initial needs to go in its own field!

3. How will the information be structured and kept up to date? For example, collecting age information in categories versus date of birth. Capturing information into categories is restrictive, because it becomes inaccurate over time. For example, with age categories you won't be able to track

people's ages over time. If instead you capture date of birth, you can always calculate and create any age category you like.

4. Keep your data up to date: on average 20% of contact data is not useable or becomes out of date in a year. Consider communications that allow a contact to update their details.

5. Consider validating and using look-up tables in your data wherever possible. For example when inputting country information, use a look-up table to avoid spelling mistakes and other user errors. Also, when entering phone numbers ensure it's only numeric data that is entered.

6. Consider how you update your data. If everyone in your office is sharing the same customer information and two people change a customer record on the same day, which one should you keep?

7. The better populated your database, the more prospects & customer insights you can gain.

We cannot stress enough how valuable your customer data is. Keeping it well managed and clean is essential for your business. We mentioned earlier in the book that we helped one client increase their revenues for one event (bums on seats) by $300,000 without increasing costs. How did we do it? By analysing the data and finding purchase patterns. We knew from the analysis who the most likely attendees were going to be and then we focussed on all prospects who fulfilled that same profile. The only reason that we were able to analyse the data was because we knew that their data was clean and captured correctly; something else that we were also responsible for implementing.

Running a Data Audit

Effective CRM requires you to bring customer information together to create a Single Customer View (SCV). This is a central store that holds all the information on a customer, prospect or supplier the company needs. In most businesses, customer information is dispersed in various systems throughout the organisation, for example in Sales, Marketing, Accounts and Customer Service systems. Bringing this information together is often a challenging task as information can be stored in different ways across each of these systems.   Before we consider bringing customer information together, we generally complete a Data Audit first. This is a process that looks for all customer information held in a business, evaluates its quality and completeness, and works out how it will come together in the SCV.

Start by defining where customer information is gathered, then look at how this data is collected, kept up to date and is structured. Who uses this data? Is all data required present or is certain customer information missing? How well are the data fields populated? Do you use data validation rules or look-up tables etc? Such as phone numbers must contain numbers only. Ensure the country field is a look–up field so they do not have to type it themselves. At this stage, also think about other data items that may be of use for future profiling and analysis, such as introducing an 'Interest' field for investors that captures interests such as BMV, Lease Option, HMO, etc.

Through a data audit of the various customer information sources, you can start determining the ideal data structure, improvements needed and best practices. You can also detail how it's going to be combined to create your SCV, and the rules you'll need to set up to ensure you have the most accurate and up-to-date version of the customer data possible.

It is important to realise not all of your data needs to be put in a CRM system. For example, marketers often load survey data that only 1% of their customers have replied to. So this means, only 1% of the data is populated in the database. This is not a good CRM practice as the data is badly populated (only 1%) and is correct only at the time it is loaded. Other information such as full financial details do not need to be stored in your CRM database either. You may wish to store a summary of all transactions and this should be good enough to allow you to interact and service your customers better.

Customer Fact

In a survey of data breaches, it was found that 47% of data breaches were caused by staff. These included loss or leakage of confidential information (35%), unauthorised access to data (32%) breach of data protection laws (25%) and a misuse of confidential information (16%) – Department for Business Innovation and Skills (DBIIS)

Interview - Rob Warlow
The Importance of Social Media

We're very aware of just how important social media is. Many businesses are starting to use various platforms as part of their CRM strategies, but as with any new technology, they are still learning how to make the best use of this media. We talked to Rob Warlow of Business Loan Services (BLS), who has been using social media effectively for a number of years.

Rob worked in banking for over 20 years in the UK and in Africa before he started his own business. Returning from a long spell overseas, he spotted a gap in the market, for a business that would work closely with business owners to help them access growth finance. Knowing that he had to re-establish his credibility in the field (having spent so much time overseas), he decided to write a business book: "I sat down to put together a book called Loan Sharp. It's up on Amazon, you can get it from WH Smith, Waterstones and if you Google Loan Sharp, you'll find it all over the place. It's a credibility tool so when people search my name, Rob Warlow, they would see the book."

There are three main aspects to BLS's activities; Firstly, they work with their clients to raise funds, secondly, they help any business experiencing problems in dealing with their bank, and thirdly, Rob and his team run seminars and workshops on raising finance. They work with many sectors, but property investors are a growing part of Rob's business – he recognises a growing appetite amongst lenders to start getting back into the commercial space as well as funding purchases and refurbishments.

Each of BLS's engagements is potentially a complex transaction, and Rob takes a consultative approach which builds good on-going relationships and he is now a trusted advisor to many of his repeat customers. It's that repeat business that Rob aims for but as finance isn't something that most businesses need on a regular basis, his challenge is to stay on his clients' radar. For this, he uses a number of communication strategies, starting with regular email newsletters letting customers know what BLS are up to as well as providing news and tips on business finance.

Rob discovered YouTube a few years ago and could immediately see the potential. He started posting short videos of his seminars, and then created his own channel for a regular Friday Business Finance Bulletin which he presents. He keeps them short and snappy: "Every Friday I issue my Friday Business Finance Bulletin which is a five to eight minute video blog of finance related news and finance raising tips for business owners. It's only short - five to eight minutes - because that's about the attention span that we have." He then uses email and his twitter feed to let his customers know about the new bulletin.

This works with the book to raise awareness and reinforce his expertise in the sector, but also has other advantages: "You can get a certain element of personality across in the blogs in the way you present your information and your views on the world, but there's nothing like seeing somebody talking at you through a camera." A third part of this strategy is his use of the web - he also writes a regular blog that can be found on the BLS website: http://businessloanservices.co.uk/blog/.

A lot of BLS's new customers come from referrals, but regardless of where the lead comes from, Rob's approach is to establish the confidence of prospects early on: "It means that when I go into a meeting, it's either because I've been referred by somebody and therefore my credibility is established there, or because they have gone on to their favourite search engine, had a look around for finance and found us that way. In each case we've been able to establish our credibility through these online and social media methods, and we can move on quickly because we have got over the credibility barrier".

In addition Rob uses Twitter. "I like Twitter for the immediacy of it. It's very succinct, no fluffiness. We put our tweets together pointing to our YouTube videos or blogs that we've written or retweeting other bits of information I find useful. It's something that you can react to there and then." He emphasises the importance of regular usage: "I have a whole bank of pre-written tweets which I'll put out on a regular basis to make sure I'm regularly on Twitter."

As for the other well-known social media platforms, Rob says: "I use LinkedIn and a little bit of Facebook. Facebook's not really where my target market sits. I'm very careful what I put on LinkedIn just to make sure that it's focussed on our target market and 'on message'. I do that with Twitter too." Exposure on social media and search engines has other advantages too: "I've done a few interviews on BBC

Radio about finance related issue and they've hunted me out to do that because of the book and my on-line presence".

Rob hasn't forgotten the power of one-to one communication either; "Every six to nine months I just pick up the phone to clients for a chat just to see how things are going."

As for results, Rob is putting in place a more structured measurement process, but he knows from anecdotal feedback that his social media strategy is already having results; "Very regularly I will get a call from a client saying, 'I watched your video this morning. It reminded me to give you a call.' Seeing the video that day prompted them to pick up the phone." But generally he uses social media to raise awareness; "For me, our focus in social media marketing is really around awareness and to make sure that we are top of mind. The moment somebody says, 'I need finance' then the next thought has to be, Rob Warlow and the Business Loan Services team."

When we asked Rob what he was planning next he replied "I do a lot of travelling in the car. What better place to stick on a business show or sales marketing podcast, whatever it may be? That's something else that I'm toying with at the moment before we move on to that as well".

He's also not ruled out more traditional methods as part of his marketing efforts "We're toying with the idea at the moment of also going out with a printed newsletter once a quarter. A couple of weeks ago, one had dropped into my letter box and I found myself sitting and reading it. I suspected that if I'd received that as a PDF attachment to an email I probably would have just deleted it. I'm starting to think there's a space there and sometimes things go around in a full circle."

We asked Rob for a final piece of advice for any business owner looking to start using social media: "Just get out there and do it. I look back over my journey and I know there are many things that I should have done which I didn't because of a perceived fear behind the technology or finding the time to take a particular action. Sometimes I look back and think, 'I should have started that particular aspect a lot sooner.' But there are times when you have to recognise that you may not have the necessary skills and so the answer is to get somebody in who does understand how to do it. I should probably have outsourced a lot more than I did, not only to bring in experts, but also to relieve myself of some mundane, non-core tasks."

CRM Technology - Types of CRM Systems

"You've got to start with the customer experience and work back towards the technology – not the other way round." – Steve Jobs

As they say: "Now here's the science". Some sort of IT system is almost always a key part of introducing CRM to a business so we thought we'd take a chapter to look at the question of CRM systems and technologies; although as we've said before, do not start with the technology as there is no need to. There are enough CRM systems and technologies out there and it is important that the system you choose matches your requirements and not the other way around. The risk is too great and we have seen many companies end up trying to fit square pegs into round holes as a result – something that doesn't work well.

Making an effective CRM strategy happen in any modern business will need tools - usually a CRM technology platform. We see the technology as only a tool; it takes the strategy, people and activities as well to create a workable CRM vision. If any part of the vision is weak, or if they are poorly matched, your CRM initiative is likely to fail.

Types of CRM Systems

Many CRM systems come with claims that they will support every requirement a business has. Here's a quick run-down of the main types of systems available – all calling themselves CRM in some form or another:

Marketing Automation / Campaign Management

These systems offer functionality aimed at businesses running marketing campaigns. They will usually include the ability to import and manage external lists (purchased or leased data) in a database, make selections based on the data held, and create campaigns using mail, email, phone etc. Many will support multi-touch campaigns (a series of communications such as email 1,2,3 etc) and will usually offer standardised email templates, standardised response reporting and basic data management. These tend to maintain a full history of what communication a person has received.

Call Centre

Call centre systems will be aimed at supporting telephone based marketing and customer service functions, both in-bound and out-bound. Again based around a standard database structure, the system will optimise dialling, support scripted calls, allow call logging, management & reporting, and allow users to generate follow-up actions. There is usually integration of basic customer information so that the caller has immediate access to the relevant customer details.

Salesforce Management

CRM systems aimed at supporting the activities of a sales team are known as Sales Force Automation (SFA) systems. These systems will allow the creation of leads and opportunities, and help sales staff manage those through to a closed sale. Functionality will include allocation of leads to territories, management of a contact's details, tracking of activities and management and reporting (including pipeline forecasting). They will also often offer basic marketing capabilities so that the Sales team can send out targeted specific communication that is then logged against the contact.

Email Marketing Systems

Email marketing systems support the creation of electronic marketing – usually outbound. This will involve selecting data for a communication from a database, preparing the contents of emails, sending the email out, and reporting on results. These often provide email templates, the ability to store groups of data and make the sending of emails fast and efficient.

Web/Mobile

As e-Commerce becomes the default sales channel for many businesses, so a web sales platform forms a core system. Many now have add-on modules for marketing use, giving some CRM functionality. The huge increase in the use of smartphones and tablets by customers is something that cannot be ignored by any successful business, and more and more CRM systems are offering mobile applications ('Apps') to suit.

Multi-Competency System

A multi-competency system is one that manages all key marketing, sales and customer service functions. It should offer seamless integration between the various business areas. While these systems take more effort to learn, they allow for full customer and prospect management from one system. The providers often claim to allow the software to be modified to meet the needs of each department, but in reality most businesses will find they are making slight changes in their internal processes and practises to adopt the systems' templates and business process models provided.

Customisation Vs Configuration

By 'Customisation' we mean significant changes that are made to a system specifically to meet the needs of a particular business. 'Configuration' on the other hand involves using flexibility already contained in the system to allow it best to meet the businesses' requirements. There are many risks with the former; essentially the further any system is moved from its standard set up, the higher both installation and on-going costs will be. Future upgrades also become more challenging to implement. This is an area requiring companies to make complex decisions balancing these risks and costs against the overheads of implementing business process changes, and most mid-sized businesses will need specialist help to make that decision. There are many CRM systems out there that allow easy configuration and these tend to be a better fit for smaller companies.

On-Premise vs SaaS (Software as a Service)

Traditionally, a business would hold and maintain their own computer systems (known as on-premise) or have them managed and run by a specialist IT hosting supplier; where the software supplier (vendor) and the hosting companies would be separate companies. With SaaS, a cloud based CRM solution, users access the system using browser based tools either through their desktop or mobile, not software loaded onto their laptops or PCs. None of the software is held on the businesses' own machines, and the supplier hosts both the software and the businesses' data. The advantages of this are usually cost and speed of implementation; a small business with straightforward needs might be up and running literally within hours of appointing a supplier. We recently tested a cloud based CRM system for a client of ours. From never seeing it before, then loading data, making data selections, setting up a multiple campaign (that included email and text) and getting the reporting back took less than 2 hours! There are some wonderful cloud based CRM systems out there to support your CRM strategy.

Integration Issues

Very few computer systems can run in isolation to the other IT platforms within a business. A CRM system might need to 'talk' to an existing order processing system, an invoicing system, or an e-commerce platform or website. Making two or more systems work seamlessly with each other can be difficult, expensive and time-consuming. Additionally, a new CRM system might need to take data from existing systems. This communication process can be automated – usually using standardised interfaces – but each will require effort and management, and can often give rise to issues when, for example, two systems hold conflicting information. This is an area that needs careful consideration as it can cause difficulties when a CRM system is introduced.

There is much more information to share on the technology aspects of CRM and far too much content to include in this book. **If you would like to know more about CRM systems or would like a list of the latest CRM systems that are available for small, medium and large companies, please email us at marketing@focus2020. Be sure to send us your name and number. Alternatively, further contact details can be found at the back of this book.**

Customer Fact
The tipping point of on-premise versus SaaS-based CRM deployments is arriving in 2015 and SaaS deployments will reach a maximum of 80% to 85% by 2025. – Gartner.

Interview - Lee Nicholls

Utilising Customer Systems Effectively in Business

Unlike many investors, Lee has always been involved in the property business. When he was a teenager, Lee gave up the chance of a prestige apprenticeship with Ford to start working as a roofer in Wales. Within a couple of years he was working on his own as a roofing sub-contractor, and not long after that had started a building business. Success came rapidly, and he gradually put more of the resources of the business into building his own portfolio of rental properties.

Eventually, after years of working seven days a week, and at the age of 39, Lee decided to retire. It didn't last long, as he realised that most of his friends were still working during the day, and were not around: "It was a lonely world because not too many people could come out to play!"

Lee discovered he still had the drive and determination to start again. He now runs one of the biggest private property businesses in Wales. There are two parts to the organisation, the first is a rental business managing a large portfolio of properties and offering various associated services such as estate agency and property sourcing, the second is an investment business, offering opportunities to investors looking to enter the Welsh market. In his own words: "We provide the complete range of services, from the buying to the facilitating of the financing; whatever that property needs in relation to its purchase, finance, sale and refurbishment."

Lee is in no doubt of the importance of customers to the success of any business: "They are the most important thing to the business; they are the lifeblood of the business. I think one thing I would always say is that it's not about you, it's about the customer. We are important but we're nowhere near as important as the customer."

Lee also recognises that the property business can be quite different to many others, revolving as it does around something that is so important to the lives of many people: "You're dealing with the most important thing in the world, their home so the intensity level is sky high."

It's that recognition which he feels is the secret to the success of his Property Plus, and the willingness of him and his team to go the extra mile on behalf of their customers: "We try to deliver the full aspect of property which is the property, the financing, the conveyancing and as much as help as possible to complete what is to most people super-duper stressful. So for example we will really hound the solicitors and IFAs to work as hard as they can for our investors."

He goes on: "You've got to think of selling a million pound house and give customers the services of a million pound house sale for a thousand pound sale." A customer-led CRM approach to running a large complex business like Property Plus needs support from systems. We asked Lee what systems they use: "We have a massive system which we've developed over a lifetime. It has the facility to log everything against the people, the property, and the solicitor". That's crucial to Lee's ability to respond to his customer when they contact him: "If the customer phones up, we should be able to answer any questions, and deliver the documentation, the conversations and correspondence the customer needs".

His communication strategy reflects the importance Lee places on respecting his customers; "I do like verbal communication." But he's also realistic to know that relying on conversations has its pitfalls: "Some people only hear what they want to hear so to get that clarity, it has to go into the system and has to be sent to the client. I find the postal system atrocious and I always like to email; email has a stronger chance of getting there rather than the post".

The system has a secondary purpose, something that many people with a portfolio of properties will recognise "If we get into a situation where we could end up in a court of law, we have to prove everything that has taken place because hearsay is no good to anybody. We've been to court several times and have been proven 100% correct every single time, the system being able to deliver all of the information we need; time and date stamped."

When it comes to new methods of communication, Lee is already using Twitter (find him on @propertygift) to inform his followers of new opportunities on the market as they come up as well as news items of interest to investors.

Meeting Lee was a very interesting experience for us. It is great to meet someone working in the industry that is so determined not to lose sight of how important his customers really are to his business. We'll leave the last word to him: "Treat people how you want to be treated, I think that is the base code of everything".

What Next?

"A customer is the most important visitor on our premises. He is not dependent on us. We are dependent on him. He is not an interruption to our work. He is the purpose of it."
– Mahatma Gandhi

We hope that we have shared enough information in this book to give you a good understanding of what CRM is and to get you started on your CRM journey. It is not an easy path and you will have to re-think how you operate your business. But believe us, it is well worth it! If implemented correctly, the benefits to your business can be massive. We have come across companies that have a 50% churn rate (customers leaving) which is far too high. By helping them bring their churn rate down, we were able to increase their overall business profitability by over 20%.

The goal of CRM is to build meaningful relationship with your customers in order to build a loyal customer base. Think of it this way, if you have a 100 customers and each one recommends one person who buys, you have doubled your business. The sales cycle will be shorter (as the prospect has come from recommendation) and your customers are likely to be happier.

Below are the main actions that will give you the best chance of success when implementing CRM:

1. Start with your business requirements and define your CRM strategy first.

2. Speak to your current customers, prospects, suppliers and staff. Listen twice as hard as speaking.

3. Evaluate your current communication and product / service delivery mechanisms. What does the customer experience look like? Are there any gaps and if so, how can you fill them?

4. Consider data. What information are you collecting about your customers? Are you collecting 'snapshot in time' data where it is only relevant at that point in time? Are you collecting information that remains consistent throughout such as collecting 'date of birth' rather than 'age'? Are you collecting the same information, in the same structure from every 'touchpoint' such as 'interest area' and so on? Remember, the data you collect about your customers and prospects is incredibly valuable and over time, will provide you with intelligence that will help you surpass your competitors.

5. Think about measurement. What metrics do you want to monitor in your business? Decide this at the beginning as you may not have all of the relevant information right now to produce the reports and you may need to start collecting it.

6. Get the right tools that match your CRM strategy. Do not try to match your CRM strategy to your tools as you will end up compromising and there is no need to do that. There are hundreds of good CRM tools out there, some better for sales and lead management and others better for marketing automation. Some suit large companies and others SMEs. There is a considerable amount of information available online and finding the right tools shouldn't be too difficult. **We keep a list of our favourites and so if you get really stuck, get in touch and we'll share what we have.**

7. Keep measuring and tweaking your CRM strategy. To achieve the best results, keep monitoring the effectiveness and adjust where necessary. Don't forget to get regular feedback from those that you frequently interact with.

8. **Enjoy the journey and the rewards that follow!**

One of our favourite brands that has consistently embraced the concept of the 'customer experience' is Apple. We'll leave the final thoughts on where to begin to Steve Jobs:

"You've got to start with the customer experience and work back towards the technology – not the other way round." – Steve Jobs

Interview – Sunil C Patel
Keeping Your Customers Happy

Far from being born with a silver spoon in his mouth, Sunil Patel grew up in a tough neighbourhood in West London. He's now a property millionaire and the Director of London Achievers, a training company for entrepreneurs.

Sunil's early entrepreneur journey taught him lessons that he's never forgotten; to keep expenses low and assets high. When his friends were driving flashy cars Sunil put all he's cash into property and those same friends regret it now.

When Sunil meets people with limited resources he says "It doesn't mean that they're below a millionnaire. Money never changes your core character". Sunil respects people for their integrity and character never wealth.

Sunil managed to buy his first property at the age of 23, but his ambitions emerged long before that; "From as long as I can remember I set a goal to make a million pounds." Without a regular job, any savings and with his age and credit history counting against him, Sunil found it very tough to get a mortgage on his first property – an ex-council flat in White City. "I got declined by so many mortgage lenders." Sunil refused to give up and finally got his mortgage approved after being declined 10 times previously. Sunil still remembers the bank manager's name - Mark Shilloto. Sunil says the only reason he got the mortgage was because of his enthusiasm and passion. He remembers the bank manger repeatedly asking "Are you sure you can handle the mortgage" and himself answering "Yes I can". After securing the mortgage Sunil had a second hurdle of raising the deposit funds and having no other alternative, he used his full university student grant to fund the purchase.

That property increased in value by £10,000 within 12 months, and Sunil dropped out of university. He worked hard clearing all his debts and started a millionaire plan to acquire one more property each year; "I used to save my money from two jobs. I used to borrow money from my sister, my friends and my uncle."

The growth in his portfolio enabled him to meet that early ambition: "I hit my target of a million pounds in twelve years - I told my close family & friends saying 'You didn't know this but I had a goal to make a million pounds from nothing and today – I've hit the million pound mark on paper.' The strange thing is, after that, the initial excitement lasted for about a couple of months; then it just fizzled out, and I carried on as an un-motivated property investor. It was the excitement of the Goal, the journey which pushed me. It was never about the money."

Currently Sunil has over twenty properties in London, Dubai and Spain. Sunil now focuses on property developing and his business 'London Achievers Ltd' which he launched globally training Entrepreneurs. London Achievers emerged after Sunil started attending various entrepreneurial events, where he met many people who had taken lots of courses but were unhappy with the value they got in return for their investment; "I thought to myself, I need to set up my own training company to help others and that is where London Achievers was born."

It's generating that customer satisfaction that's important to Sunil. When we asked him what Customer Relationship Management meant to him he replied; "Making sure the customers are happy. The customer has to be happy, number one – it's the most important thing. If the customer's not happy, your business can't grow to global levels." Interested in exploring the idea of customer satisfaction closer we asked if there was any companies that, in his view, executed CRM really well: "Virgin. I know if I'm phoning up Virgin or using their services, the staff will be genuinely happy, helpful and professional and will follow-up. Another great example is Starbucks – their staff all seem genuinely determined to give great service to their customers".

It's a lesson Sunil carries through to his own property business; "If a tenant phones you with a problem, deal with it. Don't moan, because if you don't deal with it, they're going to go and live somewhere else". He picked up another lesson from understanding Virgin's approach: "I learned this from Richard Branson; don't make enemies in business. Sometime you might have a falling out with a council worker or a builder - it will happen, we can't help it, we're human after all. But what I've learnt is always try to leave it with a nice atmosphere. A couple of weeks after the incident, give them a phone call, take them out for coffee – even if you don't want to, forgiveness is important because otherwise your vital energies can be drained"

We asked Sunil how he uses social media to deliver the sort of customer care he admires: "I use all social media platforms. I genuinely like to inspire people & make them have light bulb moments and social media facilitates this. After an event or a property conversion, I post photographs and videos on social media of my projects to educate people and expand my brand." Whilst Sunil states that he firmly believes in face to face / word of mouth marketing, he agrees that that social media accelerates customer reach immensely; "Just ask Mark Zuckerberg".

When we asked Sunil what the three key learnings he would share with someone starting a business he replied: "Number one, whatever business you're in, find the best in your industry and emulate. So if you were starting a small cafe business, I'd say, visit the best, most successful cafe in your area that's very busy, go and sit inside there, have a coffee, watch the environment; and learn exactly what's made this business successful, then replicate what they're doing."

"The second thing is to train yourself in business intelligence, train yourself in profit and loss, read Atuksha's book – and train yourself to be a business person. Don't think that just having a good business idea automatically makes you money. Train yourself in customer relations, stock-taking, branding, marketing, the way the shop should look and so on. When I studied what makes billionaires successful, I discovered that they work on productive tasks and delegated and systemised the rest. It's important to know daily profits and all the key information about your business."

My third tip is for goodness sake, make sure your customers are happy! Making money is a people thing – because your business is nothing without the customers being happy. You need to do market research. For example when your customers are leaving, ask them for their opinions. Honestly, what do you think? How could I improve it? How could I make your experience in my business better? It's essential to work backwards from the customer's needs and then produce your product or service.

And finally, I'd say set massive, exciting goals! This is important because when the going gets tough you can push through. You won't see it as work and you will go the extra mile when required. Never give up."

The Prince's Trust and Focus 2020

"The biggest risk is not taking any risk. In a world that's changing really quickly, the only strategy that is guaranteed to fail is not taking risk." – Mark Zuckerberg

Why we are Supporting The Prince's Trust

Over a year ago, Atuksha was introduced to some of the team at the Prince's Trust Cymru and some of the young people that they are helping. Listening to the stories of the young people and seeing what they have achieved, in some cases, in the face of adversity, was truly inspiring.

Taking the first steps to setting up a business or inventing a product or making the decision to create a better future for yourself can be daunting. It can be a lonely place for many and these young people take the initiative day in day out to create a better future for themselves and those around them.

This is a very worthy cause and will shape a better future for many young people. We are very proud to be able to provide support.

About The Prince's Trust

The Prince's Trust supports 13 to 30 year-olds who are unemployed and those struggling at school and at risk of exclusion. Many of the young people helped by The Trust are in or leaving care, facing issues such as homelessness or mental health problems, or have been in trouble with the law. The Trust's programmes give vulnerable young people the practical and financial support needed to stabilise their lives, helping develop self-esteem and skills for work. Since 1976,

---

Cave to Castle

The Prince's Trust has helped more than 800,000 young people and supports over 100 more each day. Three in four young people supported by The Prince's Trust move into work, education or training.

In Wales alone, The Prince's Trust supports over 3,000 young people each year, many of whom have been stuck in long-term unemployment. The impact of being out of work for an extended period of time can be devastating for young people, breeding feelings of worthlessness, low self-esteem and even depression. Research conducted by The Trust revealed that more than half of unemployed young people feel anxious about everyday situations with many avoiding meeting new people and struggling to make eye contact. This not only has an impact on the social interactions of young people, it also affects their general health. Worryingly, more than a third of unemployed young people say that anxiety has stopped them from eating properly and many even find it difficult to leave the house.

The Trust runs a variety of courses to tackle these issues, providing unemployed young people with invaluable experience that doesn't only improve their future job prospects, but also boosts their confidence and self-worth. These include a structured 12-week personal development course, intensive get into work schemes and short engagement programmes designed to inspire young people and help them move forward in their lives. The Trust works with employers in a wide range of industries to provide young people with vocational experience to help them move into employment at the end of each course. The Trust believes in providing each young person with individual guidance and support to ensure the course they participate in is appropriate to their needs. Each young person is also given post-programme support to help them move into sustainable employment in the future. In 2014, 77% of young people who completed a Prince's Trust course in Wales moved into employment, education, training or long term volunteering.

The Prince's Trust also helps young people to set up in business, providing start-up funding, training and the support of a business mentor to offer advice every step of the way. From beauticians to barbers, digital agencies to dog grooming, The Trust has helped more than 80,000 young people to realise their dream of working for themselves.

In addition to helping young people get into work, The Trust reaches out to those who are struggling in school and at risk of exclusion with a number of programmes designed to help students re-engage with education. This includes the XL course which uses experiential learning to support young people to develop a range of personal, educational and employability skills.

The Prince's Trust prides itself in being an approachable and diverse organisation which values and respects people's different backgrounds, characteristics, ideas and beliefs. It is responsive to the needs of young people, staff, volunteers, delivery partners and all stakeholders.

Thousands of young people learn the hard way but thanks to support from The Trust, they are able to realise their potential. Further information about The Prince's Trust is available at princes-trust.org.uk or on 0800 842 842.

About The Authors and Focus 2020

"We are what we repeatedly do. Excellence, then, is not an act, but a habit." – Aristotle

Atuksha Poonwassie

Atuksha is the owner of Focus 2020. Since May 2000 when the company was formed, Atuksha has been providing Customer Relationship Management guidance and support to businesses across many industries and across all regions. Atuksha enjoys exploring and resolving customer engagement challenges. She is passionate about working with businesses to increase profits whilst building better long-term relationships. She believes that a directed communication plan, regardless of channel, is vital to maintaining a loyal customer and prospect base.

Being a firm believer in the use of data across the business, Atuksha provides solutions that exploit data to its full potential. She believes that the data held within many businesses holds immense value but is very often underused. She is also a big fan of implementing simple but effective solutions that adapt to business change - quickly.

On the property front, Atuksha has been investing for over 10 years and with her husband, has a small portfolio of properties in Kent, Wales and France. She has also project managed significant builds and bought empty properties back to life, creating homes for families.

"I love both CRM and the property marketplace. Having supported some very large companies with their CRM implementations and then on-going targeting and profiling of their customers, I decided to focus my attention on the SME space. Having spoken to many property business owners, I could instantly see the opportunity for growth by making small shifts to business processes and focusing more on the customer. CRM is also misunderstood in this marketplace and I wanted to share my knowledge and experience of CRM with my colleagues and friends. I truly believe that by implementing CRM early within a business the business will grow much faster and will be built on much more stable foundations. This doesn't mean buying expensive tools and systems which in many cases are not suited to the business."

Outside of work, Atuksha loves travelling, in particular, exploring different cultures and seeing wildlife. She is also a fixed wing pilot and practices Aikido and Yoga.

Cave to Castle

Charles Eaton-Hennah

Charles specialised in marketing data, operations and CRM technology after a number of more general marketing roles. His experience in senior roles at agency, client and vendor organisations means he has seen most of the challenges marketers face first hand.

He's convinced that even now, a decade or more after the 'CRM revolution', a lot of companies still don't do the data side of marketing very well. The ability of mail, web, social media and mobile technology to generate large amounts of data mean there's no excuse not to know your customers, yet a lot of marketing communications are still irrelevant and essentially untargeted. Marketing data technology tools have now dropped in price to the point where they are affordable for any organisation. Harness their power for the heavy lifting, introduce effective processes, get intelligent with your analysis, and suddenly it's simple to start generating value from your marketing budget, instead of worrying about execution.

After heading up a global team at Gartner, Charles left to set up a consultancy, working with numerous clients to support marketing operations strategy and programmes, both large scale projects and smaller initiatives. His recent engagements have included 8 months in Hong Kong working with an international financial services company, spells in the US on a healthcare project, and a contract at the UK's biggest integrated marketing agencies.

Home for Charles and his family is under the big skies close to shingle beaches of the West Sussex coast.

His other interests are wide; from music, travel, architecture, history and books. Charles has a keen eye for property and built one of his previous homes in Windsor. His other passions involve anything that moves, has an engine or makes a noise, and a large motorbike and an old Porsche conspire to keep him poor. His heroes are Jimmy Clark, Patrick Leigh Fermor and TE Lawrence.

Haico Van Der Steen

Haico is a strategic marketer and CRM professional, driven by improving CRM and marketing strategies and delivering commercial results. He has worked in senior roles within the travel and telecommunications industry before moving into marketing and CRM consultancy on an international basis.

He believes in using customer data to deliver a better Return On Investment (ROI) on marketing spend and to increase customer profitability. He's still amazed that organisations are willing to spend vast amounts of money on acquiring new customers, yet at the same time leave their back door wide open for (the most profitable) customers to leave. Through analysis and segmentation, companies can set up a customer value management strategy to ensure customers remain loyal and hence, raise profitability substantially.

Early on in his career Haico started as a marketing analyst, but soon climbed his way up into Marketing Management and Director Level. Since the millennium Haico has been working as a consultant for major brands in the travel and telecommunications industry all over Europe and in the Caribbean and South America.

He's also involved in the property business, currently building a yoga and meditation retreat in Portugal, specialising in Cancer recovery patients. He loves being in the middle of nature and his hobbies include travelling, walking, cycling and swimming. He is a PADI Divemaster and he loves to lay in the middle of a shoal of fish somewhere in a clear blue sea. No surprise then that he is a keen on nature conservation.

About Focus 2020 Limited

Focus 2020 is a specialist, independent Customer Relationship Management (CRM) Consultancy that helps businesses find, acquire and keep loyal customers. Our goal is to help business owners understand the value of their customers and to help them build long-term relationships in order **to increase profits, increase business efficiencies, reduce costs and reduce churn**.

The Focus 2020 team have over 40 years' worth of CRM experience and have worked with some of the world's best known brands as well as with some niche small businesses and property entrepreneurs. This is across all industry sectors and across all regions.

We love what we do and will only work with businesses where we know we can make a positive difference.

What Others Say About Us

"Thank you to Atuksha and her great team for the continued CRM support provided to Limbcare. Using the principals, processes and technology ideas shared in this book, we know that our charity will go from strength to strength and will allow us to build better, long-term relationships with our supporters, clients and volunteers."

Ray Edwards, MBE, Chairman, Limbcare | Inspirational Speaker

"Everything Atuksha does is people focussed and about creating and nurturing meaningful relationships. The result of this desire to always serve people better is that she appears to have the Midas touch. I couldn't think of a better person to learn from!"

Duncan CJ, Spirt Pig

More About The Contributors

"Traditional corporations, particularly large-scale service and manufacturing businesses are organised for efficiency. Or consistency. But not joy. Joy comes from surprise and connection and humanity and transparency." – Seth Godin

There are many wonderful people who have provided us with their invaluable insight and feedback that has been shared in this book. To find out more about them, please see below.

Kevin Green
Company: Kevin Green Wealth
Website: http://www.kevingreen.co.uk
Book Title: The Rich Rules, Steps to wealth and happiness

Shaa Wasmund MBE
Company: SW Media Enterprises
Website: http://www.shaa.com/
Book Title: Do Less, Get More. How to work smart & live life your way

Simon Zutshi
Company: Property Investors Network
Website: http://www.pinmeeting.co.uk | http://www.property-mastermind.co.uk
Book Title: Property Magic, How to buy property using other people's time, money and experience

Davin Poonwassie

Company: Simple Backing

Website: http://SimpleBacking.co.uk/ | http://www.SimplePropertyApp.com/

Book Title: Simple Crowdfunding, Learn the secrets to crowdfunding success

John Lee and Vincent Wong

Company: Wealth Dragons

Website: http://wealthdragons.com/

Book Title: The Wealth Dragon Way, The why, the when & the how to become infinitely wealthy

Keith Penny

Company: Pennymatters

Website: http://www.pennymatters.co.uk

Juswant and Sylvia Rai

Company: Berkshire Property Meet (BPM)

Website: http://www.berkshirepropertymeet.com

Contact Number: +44 (0) 7748 100018

Dan Latto

Company: Daniel Latto Coaching

Website: http://www.daniellatto.co.uk/

Rob Warlow

Company: Business Loan Services

Website: http://businessloanservices.co.uk

Contact Number: +44 (0) 8456 809728

Book Title: Loan Sharp: Get the business finance you deserve

Lee Nicholls

Company: Property Plus Wales

Website: http://www.propertypluswales.co.uk

Sunil C Patel

Company: London Achievers

Website: http://www.londonachievers.com

Contact Number: +44 (0) 7947811694

Book Title: Student Loan Millionaire (release date TBC)

The Prince's Trust Cymru

Website: http://www.princes-trust.org.uk

Contact Number: +44 (0) 800 842 842

Authors: Atuksha, Charles and Haico

Company: Focus 2020

Website: http://www.focus2020.co.uk

Ray Edwards MBE

Charity: Limbcare

Website: http://www.limbcare.org/ | www.rayinspires.org

Contact Number: +44 (0) 800 052 1174

Book Title: I'm Still Standing

Duncan CJ

Company: Spirit Pig

Website: http://www.SpiritPig.com

Our Final Thoughts

"The only limit to your impact is your imagination and commitment." – Anthony Robbins

Imagine a barge that is being pulled by many tugboats. If each tugboat pulls in a different direction, the barge will not go anywhere and it will be wasted effort by everyone involved. Eventually, those controlling the tugboats will get disheartened and give up. But what if all of those tugboats had a plan and were working together to pull that barge in a certain direction. What do you think will happen? The barge will reach it's intended destination. This is what CRM achieves. It allows all departments (tugboats) to work together to help the barge (your business) reach it's intended destination.

If implemented correctly, CRM can supercharge your business but at the same time build stable foundations for growth. It will create a happy and fulfilling business that is built upon great relationships, streamlined consistent business processes and an environment where everyone within the business is working towards the same goals.

Having helped businesses with their CRM challenges over many years, we know what works and what doesn't. If you start with the technology or tools, there is a high chance that your CRM implementation will not deliver. Start with your business objectives and define your CRM strategy. Then spend time on your data. Only when you have these in place should you consider the technology. Don't fall into the 'square peg, round hole' trap. We cannot stress this enough.

There are many other aspects to CRM such as data analytics and profiling, event-trigged marketing, sales pipeline management, customer service and call centre integration etc. that have not been covered here. Our goal for this book is to provide an introduction to CRM, provide our views on the most important aspects of CRM and provide insight from the amazing people who have shared their views about CRM and the Importance of Customers. We believe that we have achieved this but would love to hear your thoughts and feedback.

And finally, enjoy your CRM journey. It will be amazing. You, your customers, your staff, your suppliers and your business will be much happier and better off for it.

To your Success! With warmest wishes, Atuksha, Charles and Haico.

Cave to Castle's Success

Within a week of launching the book on Kindle, 'Cave to Castle' hit Amazon #1 Bestseller for Business Skills, something that we are very proud of. We are also fortunate to have our book seen in many places including: